# THE CASE FOR De GAULLE:

## AN AMERICAN VIEWPOINT

# THE CASE FOR
# DE GAULLE:

## AN AMERICAN VIEWPOINT

*By* John L. Hess

WILLIAM MORROW AND COMPANY, INC.

New York 1968

# CONTENTS

# NOTES ON A REVOLUTION

*"Nothing will ever again be quite the same."*
*—Premier Georges Pompidou, addressing*
*National Assembly on May 22, 1968.*

AMONG THE THINGS that will never be the same, after
the stunning, frightening, and exhilarating French upheaval
of May, 1968, are Franco-American relations. I don't know
how it all looked from abroad, but some American and British
periodicals that occasionally found their way to Paris during
the crisis offered this impression: first, a deep satisfaction that
at last de Gaulle was getting his comeuppance; then, a growing
feeling of alarm that a major Western nation—one of *us*, after
all—was sliding into anarchy and communism; finally, relief
that the *existing order* had, after all, survived in recognizable
form. It was wryly amusing to read commentaries hailing the
Gaullist election victory, written by men who had not had a
kind word for France since 1962. One thing that has not
changed, it would seem, is their predilection for being wrong
about de Gaulle. They berate him when he is admirable; they
embrace him when he is deplorable.

To be fair, they have no monopoly on error. What the
French now call *les évènements* ("the events," or shall we say
"happenings"?) came as a total surprise to everyone, including
the handful of students who set them off. A few weeks earlier,

one of the nation's finest journalists had published a critique of his apathetic countrymen under the headline, "France Is Bored . . ." Like other newsmen, I had myself reported that French students had so far failed to respond to the unrest that was sweeping the campuses of the world.

This book, a modest effort to lessen American hostility toward France by explaining the French side of our quarrels, was completed a few days before the explosion of May. Turning back to it now, I find embarrassing to read my description of France as, thanks to de Gaulle, a stable and prosperous land, living in peace at home and abroad and enjoying the highest prestige in the Third World. On reflection, I have decided to let these passages stand. It would be cowardly to change them; furthermore, they were true at the time and remain valid in context. What happened in France last May is significant to us precisely because she was, like us, a prosperous, expanding, democratic Western country. If her prosperity was not up to ours, she did not have a Vietnam war or a race problem to tear her people apart. If her educational system, erected under Napoleon, was far less adapted than ours to modern times, how shall we explain that Columbia University was "occupied" before the Sorbonne?

Now that it is over—for the time being—we can for the first time review what happened. A French labor reporter suggested to me that it really began with the postwar baby boom. The children born then have now come to maturity, overflowing the universities, forming a majority of employees in some new factories. It is irrelevant to say that they never had it so good, that with their cars and pocket money, they live better lives than their fathers ever knew. An older worker recounts that at a shop meeting he began to recall the experience of a strike in 1962 when he was interrupted by a young voice from the rear: "Hey, dad, are you gonna tell us about the Middle Ages?" The veteran said he did not dare mention the last great general strike here, in 1936. . . . It is also irrelevant to say, as Pompidou did, that the government had in a few years doubled the university building space and tripled the education budget. For the youth, the fact that today's reality is better than yesterday's is beside the point. It is simply not good enough.

The upheaval was a strange mixture of the absurd, the terrifying, and the inspiring. It started at the University of Paris's new annex in the working-class suburb of Nanterre, a depressing complex of concrete blocks in a mud wasteland. A few score ultraradical students began last winter to raise Cain about whatever grievances came to hand: the right of boys and girls to swap visits in the dormitories, the right to smoke in class, and finally the right to hold political meetings on campus. By the end of April, they were disrupting lectures by slamming desk lids (as deputies sometimes do in the National Assembly); the dean finally reacted by closing the school. He may have thought that a majority of students would turn on the troublemakers who were disrupting their studies at the approach of the critical year-end exams. On the contrary, the general reaction was one of admiration for the leaders and sympathetic interest in their protest. One reason was a multiplicity of obvious grievances, such as overcrowding and impossible transportation problems. A more profound reason was the alienation between student and faculty. "I've never been within thirty meters of a professor," a student told me. The typical French professor lectures in a large amphitheater, often so crowded that most students registered for his course don't bother to attend, but buy mimeographed copies of his lectures instead. Until this May, a discussion between professor and students was virtually impossible.

When Nanterre was closed, its handful of Maoist, Castro-ist, Trotskyist, and anarchist students known as *les enragés* marched on the Sorbonne on May 3. There the dean took the fateful step of calling in the police to drive them out. It may be heresy to say so but, even after all that has happened, the dean's behavior does not seem to me to have been unreasonable. The *enragés* were going to close the school anyhow. What the dean could not foresee was the reaction of the student body, the police, and the community. The students instinctively rallied by the thousands against the police, and fighting broke out. Gendarmes and the CRS (Compagnies Républicaines de Sécurité), a tough riot police force, fought with clubs, teargas, and concussion grenades, the students with paving blocks and, later, Molotov cocktails. Night after night, the Latin Quarter was a battleground. Hundreds of persons were injured, including policemen, youths, and by-standers, who frequently were mauled by the police. There were many authenticated cases of beatings of prisoners in police stations.

(It should perhaps be noted that the CRS was following standing orders given by its founder, the socialist interior minister Jules Moch, after the war. These call for the use of brutality—the word is employed—to break the will of organized mobs. Americans here frequently expressed amazement that nobody was killed. It was remarkable to observe lines of French policemen armed with carbines holding their fire while being pelted with stones and bottles of flaming gasoline. It is a difference of tradition. In fighting their fellow countrymen, the French are more likely to use clubs than guns.)

The reaction of the Paris middle class was another surprise. The first clue came early when a diplomat said, "My son was in that fighting last night. I'm proud of him." The students were, after all, the children of the middle class. Everybody acknowledged that the universities needed a good shaking up. In drawing rooms and restaurants, the bourgeoisie berated the "flics."

The authorities evidently were at a loss, as well they might be. President de Gaulle normally used to leave housekeeping matters to Premier Pompidou, but that tough, shrewd Auvergnat was off in Afghanistan. The second-string ministers were divided; de Gaulle appears to have ruled for those favoring force. It didn't work. On the night of Friday, March 10, the extremist youths, now numbering thousands, raised barricades in the Latin Quarter. Paris awoke next morning to a scene of devastation, with burned cars littering torn-up streets and with lingering fumes of teargas and rubber. Everybody blamed the authorities. The Communists, who until then had treated the carryings on of the "leftists" with contempt, swung around to call a one-day general stoppage on Monday, March 13, to protest police brutality. It was the first, and only, time during the crisis when students and workers were to march together en masse. In Paris, close to a million filled the boulevards from the Gard du Nord through the Latin Quarter to the Place Denfert-Rochereau. There the *enragés* sought to lead a march on the Elysée, which would certainly have led to a violent confrontation at the Seine. The Communists refused and ordered their disciplined masses to disperse. They did, while some thousands of youths followed Daniel Cohn-Bendit to the Champs de Mars to hear him denounce the "Stalinist creeps" who were betraying the revolution. The affair sealed a divorce that was a determining element in what was to follow.

Pompidou, meanwhile, had flown back to Paris to give the government a leadership it had previously seemed to lack. He pulled the police out of the Latin Quarter, let the students occupy the Sorbonne, and told the National Assembly he was prepared, even eager, to negotiate reforms. (De Gaulle a few days later uttered the pungent phrase *"Réforme, oui; chienlit, non."* *Chienlit* means "bedsoiling." De Gaulle was far from his most eloquent during the crisis, but at least two more epigrams were to enter the annals of Gaulliana. When a visitor complained that France was reacting a bit excessively to the worldwide unrest of youth, he replied, *"La France est toujours exemplaire,"* which may be translated as "France always leads the way." In late May, when the nation was at the brink of anarchy and he suddenly called it to order, he was said, perhaps apocryphally, to have declared, *"Fin de la récréation!"* —"the play period is over.") Pompidou told the country, with justice, that the regime had built more schools than all previous regimes put together, and that it had introduced a series of reforms, over the stubborn resistance of an educational hierarchy. Now, he said, much more would be done, and quickly. But he was too late.

As he spoke, the workers of Sud Aviation at Nantes took a leaf from the students' notebook and occupied their plant, locking the management into its offices. Next day, two Renault plants followed suit, the following day, a dozen more, then hundreds, then thousands. When the third week of May began, all of French industry was paralyzed. The Communist CGT, or Confédération Générale du Travail, running to catch up, had called a general strike and, with its superior organization in place, quickly established a commanding position over a movement it had certainly not set off. This almost surely averted a major bloodletting.

Student and intellectual militants, dazzled by their success and inspired by the example of Fidel Castro, were convinced that *the* revolution was at hand. The left-wing Catholic labor federation, Confédération Française Démocratique du Travail, leaned toward the militants and posed the sharing of management as a major demand. The Communists, however, were convinced from the beginning that the country was *not* ready for revolution. This may have stemmed from the natural conservative inclinations of an established organization, but it was likely also to have reflected the fact that the Communists, although weak among the students and intellectuals, were deeply based among workers and peasants. Outsiders saw nine million workers on strike, and red and black flags flying over the Sorbonne and a score of factories. But several millions of these workers were idle only because plants had been occupied and transportation paralyzed, and millions more, engaged in the first strike of their lives, wanted only their share of the consumer society against which some students were in revolt. That week I talked to many young workers at plant gates; they were only dimly aware of the student uprising, and said they really had nothing in common with those "sons of the bourgeoisie." What they wanted was shorter hours and higher pay.

Another clue, hardly noticed at the time, was offered by two by-elections, which began on the Sunday before the general strike. In the runoffs a week later, the Gaullists *increased* their votes, in face of the helpless silence of their government. The bourgeois, sympathetic toward the students at the beginning of May, were now frightened—and so, as it developed, were most of the peasants and many workers.

Given their estimate that it was not a revolutionary situation, the Communists passed the bywords: "no provocations," "no adventures."

With some difficulty, they persuaded the workers to release plant managers from confinement. (Sud Aviation, with a strong Trotskyist element, was the last to accede.) They set up security forces and cleanup squads, and at the end were able to boast that not a machine had been damaged through the whole upheaval. A worker bragged to me that his factory had never been so clean. The price for these achievements was a brutal repulsion of the leftist students. At the start, Georges Seguy, the CGT chief, announced that "the workers don't need tutors," and he ordered plant pickets to admit no outsiders. The party by its silence even approved the government's subsequent repression of the extremists, including summary deportations of foreigners and the outlawry of leftist groups. On the other hand, it could claim credit for the fact that during the whole upheaval there was virtually no violence around the struck plants, except at Flins, where Paris students came to lend a hand, and at Sochaux, where the CFDT led resistance to police intervention.

The Communists did pose two major demands that went beyond bread and butter. These were union rights and repeal of the Social Security decrees of 1967. They go far toward explaining the force of the explosion that rocked France. Despite the long radical tradition of the working class, French employers had simply no experience of direct collective bargaining with their workers. Trade associations did negotiate wage agreements, and there was a system of elective shop councils, often dominated by union members. But union delegates and stewards as such were barred from most shops. The motto of employers was "Maître chez Moi"—"Boss in My Own House." (After the strike, however, the Federation of Young Bosses changed its name to Federation of Young Directors of Enterprise.) The same spirit had come to pervade a government that had been in power for ten years. The social-security decrees were a flagrant example.

The French cradle-to-grave welfare system was running a huge deficit. This shocked orthodox economic opinion—the kind that is unnerved by the deficit of the New York subway system. Unfortunately, that was the only kind of opinion being heard in the councils of power. The origin of the Fifth Republic, in a near coup d'etat of the army, had alienated the Left; the "betrayal" of French Algeria by de Gaulle earned him the hatred of the extreme Right. He remained with a largely conservative following and a technocratic administration that gradually adopted its leader's father-knows-best manner. "One de Gaulle is a very good thing," a conservative Frenchman told me. "A hundred de Gaulles are insupportable." A common complaint around the country—not, to be sure, original with the de Gaulle regime—was that Paris would not *listen*. The new autoroute would be built here, not there, and the new university there, not here. To use the cant phrase, there was no *dialogue*. Frequently, no doubt, the government engineers were right and the local interests wrong, but the right to be wrong is an essential safety valve in modern society. "Pay as you go" may be good economics and deficits may be bad, but it is worse to alienate a great section of the public.

The economic miracle of the Fifth Republic was based on firmly orthodox policy. Prices rose no more than about 2 percent a year, productivity more than 5 percent. Wages were not negotiated, they were announced; and they rose only a trifle faster than the cost of living.

This permitted a fine growth rate, a sound currency, and an excellent balance of payments, but it also produced a growing awareness among French workers that they were not getting their share of the pie. This was demonstrated by the presidential election of late 1965 and the legislative election of early 1967. But the government ignored the returns. In the summer of 1967, it rammed through by decree a "reform" of the social-security system that included a sharp cut in medical benefits. At the same time, it drastically raised Metro, bus, and train fares, just to make the point clear. In its defense it should be noted that the government was concerned about the tariff cuts coming on July 1, 1968, and felt it essential to hold prices down and assign a maximum of resources to investment. (French business is notoriously reluctant to invest in new machinery. The relatively low wages of their workers and the longest work week in the West may have encouraged this tendency.) However, the decrees deepened the feeling among workers that the government was hostile to them.

The explosion of mid-May sent shock waves into every segment of society, and brought to light as never before the frustrations that pervade our bright new world. Clerks in banks sat down to discuss together the meaning of life and the organization of their firms. Young doctors raided and occupied for forty-eight hours the headquarters of the medical profession, perhaps the most ossified, reactionary segment of French society. Newspaper staffs formed associations to demand, and sometimes obtain, a voice in policy. High schools and universities all over the country were "occupied" by their students, and for the first time since the Middle Ages, students and professors discussed man-to-man the reform of education and society. It was the definitive proof that, as Russell Baker was to observe, George Orwell was wrong. With all its brainwashing techniques, modern society is unable to turn mankind into robots.

A disproportionate amount of publicity has been given to the "folklore" aspect of the revolution: the barricades; the red and black flags; the seizure of the Odeon, a fine avant-garde national theater, by Cohn-Bendit and a ragtag of characters, including the nonactors of the nontheater movement. A similar group of underground movie addicts took over an art cinema house and turned it into a revolutionary film temple, showing old Buster Keaton pictures. Anarchy had its endearing aspects, producing imperishable posters and graffiti: "Imagination is power"; "Kiss your love, but hold on to your rifle"; "Mankind will be happy when the last capitalist has been hanged with the tripes of the last bureaucrat." (I prefer the amendment on a poster by Alechinsky: "When the last sociologist has been hanged by the tripes of the last psychiatrist, there will still be problems.") An anonymous genius amended the omnipresent warning on buildings around Paris, *"Défense d'Afficher"* ("Forbidden to Post Bills"), to read *"Défense d'Interdire"* ("Forbidden to Prohibit"). But this expression of absolute liberty was the Achilles heel of the student movement. It was impossible, the students felt, to bar the leather-jacket set, the famous "Katangese," from setting up shop in the Sorbonne and from taking a joyful lead in the cop fighting. The death of a police officer in Lyons was their work and helped turn public opinion against the whole movement.

But the errors of the students were, in the beginning, more than matched by the weakness and follies of the government. Its most effective ploy in mid-May was achieved against its will. The government radio and television network had covered the first week of troubles in an incredibly one-sided fashion. There was no live coverage of the fighting in the Latin Quarter, which would have shown police brutality, and there were no interviews with students. The government network, the ORTF, has a monopoly on broadcasting in France, but several private radio stations get around it by transmitting from across the borders, and they did a bangup job of reporting. A wave of shame swept the ORTF. Under the threat of a strike, the government allowed three young extremist student and teacher leaders to appear in a panel show. Their admission that they had no program for reform of the universities, but rather favored their abolition, their rejection of negotiation with the capitalist regime and their insistence upon an undefined social revolution was powerful propaganda for the regime. Pompidou was quick to realize this (on the TV screen half an hour later, he told the people, "You have seen them") but he, or de Gaulle, refused to ease his grip on the ORTF. The airwaves had always been one of the spoils of power; ministers of the Fourth Republic, too, had ruthlessly censored the news. Also, much of the press was in the hands of critics of the regime, and de Gaulle was determined to keep TV and radio as his means of reaching the public. But the cultural revolution had deeply affected the staff of ORTF, and it launched what was probably the world's first strike for honest news and the autonomy that might guarantee it.

The regime floundered. De Gaulle, on May 24, delivered what friends and foes alike received as the weakest speech of his career. It was an appeal for order coupled with a call for still another plebiscite, a referendum that would authorize his government to enact a vague program of "participation" for workers in management. If he did not win, he said, he would depart. The country began seriously considering the latter alternative. But while his chief was showing an unusual lack of vigor, Pompidou hurled himself into the breach. In a marathon weekend of negotiations at the Social Affairs Ministry at the Rue de Grenelle, he dragged a reluctant Patronat into granting the bulk of the general strike demands: a 35 percent rise in the minimum wage for industry, 56 percent for agriculture; a 10 percent basic pay increase, with more to be negotiated; a beginning of the return to the 40-hour week; restoration of half the cut in medical benefits; a rise in family allowances and a sort of Wagner Act insuring union rights in factories. It was far and away the greatest victory the French working class had won since 1936, and the union leaders, leaving the Rue de Grenelle at dawn on May 27, knew it. But the workers turned it down.

It is intriguing to speculate on what would have happened had they accepted it and marched singing back to work (though the French do not sing well, unfortunately, and the "Internationale" is less stirring when it is sung out of tune). It is certainly possible that the referendum would have lost, and de Gaulle would have ended a great career in humiliation. But the CGT leaders did not dare to try to sell the "Grenelle protocol" to the workers. A large majority doubtless would have received it with joy, but in the big factories that were the backbone of the movement, the young militants had raised their sights. Nothing but the downfall of the government would have satisfied them. Heeding the thunder on the left, the CGT chiefs presented the protocol without recommendation to the Renault workers. They hooted it down.

A stunned nation watched helplessly as the economy slipped toward disaster. Hoarding was rampant. The black market reappeared. In the absence of public transportation, the greatest traffic jams in history developed. Gasoline supplies dried up. Barricade fighting returned to the Latin Quarter. And the government seemed paralyzed. On Tuesday, May 28, François Mitterand, head of the Federation of the Democratic and Socialist Left, which had previously played virtually no role in the crisis, proposed that he and Pierre Mendès-France head a Leftist regime to take over. The following morning, de Gaulle slipped out a back gate of the Elysée Palace and vanished. It developed only later that he had flown to Germany to consult with his army commanders. At the time, his departure struck the country as definitive. For twenty-four hours, there was a vacuum at the seat of power, and the country trembled on the brink of anarchy and civil war. "Civic action committees" of the Right were forming, and called for counterrevolutionary demonstrations.

Then de Gaulle returned. In a brief and harsh speech, not the best of his career but certainly the most effective, he said that the Republic was threatened by "international totalitarianism," that he, its elected chief of state, would use all force to protect it, and that he was dissolving the National Assembly and calling new elections. In those few minutes, in the afternoon of May 30, the revolution ended. The Assembly disbanded in a bitterly symbolic scene, with the Left and the Right face to face across an empty chamber, defiantly singing the "Marseillaise" at each other. Outside, a million citizens waving the tricolor filled the Champs-Elysées from the Concorde to the Arc de Triomphe. The "party of fear" was no longer silent.

Instinctively, the country seemed to realize that it was all over. It was the end of a nightmare to some, the end of a dream to others. Industry by industry, plant by plant, workers began trooping back, generally with the Grenelle conditions and a few sous more—yet often with a sense of defeat. But the regime was taking no chances. In an effort to pick up the million or so votes of the extreme right, it freed General Salan and the last OAS terrorists still imprisoned. In a few places, underworld types and ultrarightists became Gaullists pro tem and attacked Leftist campaign workers. Pompidou, a jugular fighter, kept up a drumbeat of cynical propaganda about the Communist peril, to keep alive a climate of fear. In this, he received invaluable help from student extremists and their leather-jacket allies, who mounted new barricades in the Latin Quarter. When the police finally evacuated the Odeon, that by now seedy symbol of the cultural revolution, even sympathizers commented, "It was about time."

For all their exhilarating idealism—partly, because of it—the young revolutionaries managed (forgive the inevitable cliché) to snatch defeat from the jaws of victory. They had set the country on its ear, touched off a general strike that won the greatest labor gains in thirty-two years, unseated half a dozen ministers, brought about the dissolution of the National Assembly, forced all of thinking society into a serious reexamination, and assured a far-going reform of education. And they persuaded themselves and the country that this was a defeat. If it had not been for the treason of the Communists, they said, the social revolution would have been won—a social revolution they never got around to define. ("Of course," one of their sympathizers told me honestly, "if it *had* won, I would have been the first to leave the country.") A measure of how revolutionary the country really was, in their sense of the word, was given in the June election by the PSU (Parti Socialiste Unifié), the only party that really embraced the rebel cause. A helter-skelter splinter group of Left intellectuals, it entered three times as many candidates as in 1967, and obtained twice as many votes—about 4 percent of the total. The Left as a whole got about 40 percent, a decline of about four percentage points. Many workers who last time had voted Socialist or Communist now abstained or voted Gaullist, deciding that if the carryings on in the Latin Quarter was the revolution, they would rather keep the status quo. The uneasy unity of the Left was deeply undermined, the Socialists looking back nostalgically toward their traditional allies in the

Center, the Communists in trouble with both their right and left wings for their "peaceful road to socialism" line.

Saddest of all was the defeat of the ORTF strike. The newscasters, directors, and artists—the "creative workers"—held out to the end and faced a purge as their reward. The government seemed determined to keep the airwaves under its control, and there was only a faint hope that the noble self-sacrifice of its best employees would exert some influence on the future of the network. In other areas, the regime seemed to have drawn some of the lessons of May. In spite of its triumph, it made no move to undo the gains of labor, and it seemed likely that the "dialogue" would continue between labor and management, student and faculty, government and governed.

A dialogue between France and the United States would also seem less difficult than it was before May. Not that General de Gaulle has changed the fundamental line of his foreign policy, but his *preoccupation* with foreign policy has been suspended and his moral influence abroad diminished, and perhaps his occasionally irritating style will be muffled. France's troubles may appease some of France's critics in the English-speaking world, and may also have dramatized how much we have in common, for, to repeat, France was a rich, stable, expanding modern country, well managed by the best orthodox standards. It is to be hoped that a reexamination of these standards as applied to France will encourage a reexamination in our own country. Since foreign policy is one of the areas that need reconsidering, I hope that this willfully provocative book will serve a useful function.

—J. L. H.

Paris, July 4, 1968

# 1

# INTRODUCTION

> "Dear John:
> ". . . I had planned to drop in on you in Paris during
> my vacation this summer, but after the way Charley has
> been behaving, I've decided to go to Greece in-
> stead. . . ."
>     —from a letter sent by a New York newsman to a
> colleague in France, shortly after the coup d'état in
> Athens.

AMERICA HAS GONE out of its collective mind on the
subject of France. When congressmen denounce the president
of our ancient ally as "a mortal enemy," a "renegade friend,"
a "cynic," a "demagogue," a "homicidal lunatic" inspired by
"implacable hostility toward the United States" and "the
most ungrateful man since Judas Iscariot," they are only echo-
ing views prevailing among their electors. But if the citizens of
our democracy adopt en masse a paranoiac delusion, it can
only be because they have been poorly informed. Our newspapers, magazines, and broadcasting networks more or less
unconsciously share the popular prejudices, and it would be
a miracle if they did not convey it. The miracle has not, unfortunately, come to pass. The French point of view has been
consistently scanted, and even in the most objective journals,
the loaded word passes unperceived. (Where a friend would

be described as "steadfast," for example, France is "adamant." Her spokesmen "snipe" at our position, where a friend would merely "criticize.")

The difference between cool objectivity and hysteria was dramatized one day in late 1967 at a "background" meeting between the American press corps in Paris and Charles E. Bohlen, who had directed the embassy with restraint and distinction during five trying years. A leading correspondent said, "Mr. Ambassador, don't you think that Charley's foreign policy boils down to this: He gets up in the morning and says to himself, 'What can I do that would hurt the United States?' then goes ahead and does it?" Nobody seemed to think this an odd question. Bohlen, an old poker player, just blinked and raised his eyebrows, before replying. I quote from memory, but with his permission as to the substance:

"You know, I have talked with General de Gaulle maybe forty times over the last five years [more, in fact, than any other ambassador had], and I'll tell you:

"*I don't think he's anti-American at all.*

"Time and again, he likes to talk of power relations like solar systems. He just doesn't think a small- or medium-size country should get too close to a great power; it would get pulled into its orbit."

In other words, if de Gaulle has steered France away from the United States in recent years, it is because he felt that the United States had become so powerful as to menace France's independence. I do not think this is a complete explanation for French policy, but I think it is *one* explanation. It is supported by the fact that de Gaulle was just as emphatic about resisting *Soviet* power until 1964, and even since then has repeatedly urged East Europeans to guard their independence.

There was more than a hint of this motivation in de Gaulle's warm farewell toast to Bohlen a few months later. Referring to our two countries' "fundamental amity," he said:

No doubt that friendship may now seem to be undergoing some trials. But in the course of its history, soon to be two centuries old, it is not the first time.

For indeed it seems that there has always been one of our two countries whose instinct pulled toward moderation when the other tended to abandon it. In the various epochs when France chose to lead an adventurous life, she did not necessarily find the support of the United States; today, when the latter in its turn is particularly susceptible to the impulses of power, it is true that France does not constantly support it. Perhaps, after all, these divergences in such circumstances have contributed to world equilibrium.

De Gaulle here was gracefully recalling that when the Fourth Republic plunged France into the Algerian war and the Suez adventure of 1956, the United States put its weight against her; he implied that Gaullist France was only returning the favor when she rebuked us over Vietnam.

It was, perhaps, fairly strong understatement to say that France now "does not constantly support the United States," considering that de Gaulle had recently ordered our troops out of his country, urged a return to the gold standard, barred Britain from the Common Market, voted against Israel in the United Nations, and cried in Canada, "*Vive le Québec libre!*" In light of all that, Bohlen shocked many Americans in Paris when he said in a parting speech that his government had never questioned the *right* of France to take the positions she had. A loyal supporter of Administration policy, Bohlen was of course referring to the *legal* right. I shall go farther:

*In all the major points at issue between France and the United States, there is at least a debating case that France has a moral right to her position.*

*In all these points, the position taken by de Gaulle may arguably be in the best interest of France.*

*Most shocking of all, a close examination of each dispute suggests that the French position may conceivably be in the best interest of the United States.*

Some time in 1966, I think, it was suggested to me that I write a piece on rising anti-Americanism in France. I replied that I did not know of any. I had never encountered that gut prejudice against me as an American that a Frenchman may encounter against him in the English-speaking countries. The United States had always, in fact, been the most popular foreign country among the French.

Now, I am not so sure.

The enormous store of goodwill for Americans has been deeply eroded everywhere in Europe. The Vietnam war is of course the main reason. Through the Tet offensive of February, 1968, Europeans were reduced to tears by the scenes brought to them by American television clips. Combat in the streets, burning homes, fleeing women and children, Westmoreland laughing at the thump of mortars. On the front pages of newspapers was the picture of the Saigon police chief murdering a captive, and the words of the American captain to the Associated Press: "We had to destroy the city to save it."

For French readers, the same papers offered an added fillip: stories, from American news services, of Americans pouring French wine and perfume down drains. Their own newsmen reported that a Frenchman could not enter a taxi in New York or accept a social invitation in Washington without risk of insult. An American rabbi told a French television interviewer that he would not book a flight touching down in

France; he had no objection to a stopover in Frankfurt, he said.

This irrationality may be doing irremediable damage to the relations of two countries that should be friends, sharing as they do a passion for life, liberty, and the pursuit of happiness, or, *liberté, egalité, et fraternité.*

I am not a Gaullist, but I think Americans should know that, in the areas where we differ, there is a case for de Gaulle.

That's what this book is about.

# 2

# DE GAULLE AND THE JEWS

*"I do not think Nasser wanted war. The two divisions he sent into the Sinai on May 14 would not have been enough to launch an offensive against Israel. He knew it, and we knew it."*
*—Gen. Itzhak Rabin, Israeli chief of staff, nine months after the June war.*

THE EXTERMINATION CAMPS of the Third Reich have made it impossible to be coolly objective about anything involving the fate of Jews. In Germany, it has been said, only the innocent feel guilty. This bitter paradox should not be taken too literally, else one could acquit oneself simply by pleading guilt. What it does mean is that the shame of Auschwitz belongs to all mankind (in varying degrees, to be sure) and that it cannot be mitigated except by a recognition that mankind is capable of such crimes and by a resolution to combat them. This was of course the message of Hannah Arendt's book about Eichmann: the banality of evil, which infuriated so many righteous people who thought it took the Germans off the hook. It did not do that at all, but it did extend the indictment to all who by their silence, if nothing else, acquiesced to racism in general and thus, finally, to the extermination of the Jews. No people, I think, bear this burden of conscience more than do liberal Frenchmen, who are pro-

6

foundly aware that French policemen serving a still-popular French government rounded up tens of thousands of French Jews and handed them over to their executioners.

This feeling accounts largely for the overwhelming surge of sympathy for Israel in France during the spring of 1967. Regretfully, I must add that there was a less creditable factor: the strong prejudice against the Arabs left by the Algerian war. We thus witnessed a grotesque united front that ranged from ultrarightists, who still regard Marshal Pétain as a saint (and de Gaulle as his betrayer), to Socialists like Guy Mollet who waged and lost the war with the Algerians and who plotted the abortive Franco-British-Israeli strike against Egypt in 1956. At the height of the June crisis, processions of several thousand snaked through the streets chanting, *"Is-ra-el Vain-cra!"* and automobile horns responded with the rhythm of *Al-gé-rie Fran-çaise!* On Boulevard Haussmann, where young volunteers marched waving Israeli flags, a woman cried, "To Alexandria!" Beneath my office window, a young marcher contemptuously tossed a ball of rolled-up paper at an Arab workman. Two comrades pulled the Arab away. (It was curious to see Westerners turning their guilt feelings about Auschwitz against the Arabs, a more Semitic people and generally in a more pitiable condition today than the Jews. If the Jewish survivors of Nazism had chosen to carve a new Canaan out of Bavaria and smite any resisters hip and thigh, one would at any rate have had to acknowledge the rough justice of it.)

The irrationality of those lovely summery days in Paris is hard to believe. I recall that as I strolled past the Gare St.-Lazare in the morning of June 5, tensely silent pedestrians were grouped around the kiosks reading an extra edition of *France-Soir,* bearing the great black headline in war type:

"*L'Égypte Attaque Israel.*" Further on, I met a young American writer and grumbled something about the fat being in the fire and the insane headline in *France-Soir*. He stared at me, and stammered, "Y-you mean you think Egypt d-didn't attack?" A bit later, reading the bulletins reporting the destruction of the Arab air forces, a fellow correspondent, seasoned in Middle Eastern wars, said worriedly, "Gee, I hope it will become clear beyond any doubt that the Arabs struck first."

I held my tongue. The myth that the Jews of Israel were in imminent peril of extermination had so taken hold of even sophisticated men that no useful discussion was possible. Yet it was a myth. It was helped considerably, to be sure, by the threats of Arab propagandists, including Nasser, who on May 22 had cried, "If Israel wants war, we tell her, 'You are welcome,'" and four days later had boasted that, if Israel attacked, "our main objective will be the destruction of Israel." But this ranting was probably less effective than the insistence of Western journalists on describing the Israelis as underdogs—"two million against 100 million Arabs." A slight reference to history should have spared us that. Against greater odds, Cortez with a few hundred men broke the Aztec empire and the illiterate brigand Pizarro enslaved the Incas. The thin red line of the British Raj laid down the law for half the world during nearly two centuries. And some of the same journalists so carried away by the Arab peril had reported the easy victories of small groups of white mercenaries in Africa. They should have known that any time the troops of an Occidental society, well disciplined and strongly motivated, come up against more primitive peoples, it is the latter who are the underdogs.

Israel had, in fact, won every serious encounter with the

Arabs since the new state was born in 1947, within bound-
aries that its founders regarded as totally inadequate. These
were enlarged, first in 1948 and again, but only temporarily,
in 1956. This was the Suez affair, and it is worth recalling here
as a dress rehearsal for the 1967 "lightning war" (the more
common word "blitzkrieg" is avoided in this case by most
writers). In 1956, the issue at stake, in Western opinion, was
the Suez Canal, "lifeline of the British Empire." The empire
was gone but the lifeline must be saved at any cost. Ironically,
it was the Allied attack that resulted in choking off the
canal; the world survived, more or less, and several years later
one of my colleagues reported that the canal was being oper-
ated more efficiently under Egyptian control than it had been
under the Anglo-French Suez Canal Company. The Egyptians
had paid dearly, nonetheless, for Nasser's reckless seizure of
the canal.

The three partners in the Suez expedition acted from different motives. Prime Minister Eden presumably was worried
about the lifeline and Middle East oil. Premier Mollet, sink-
ing into the quicksand of the Algerian war, wanted to strike
at the fountainhead of Arab nationalism.* So, doubtless, did
Premier Ben-Gurion, but their basic objectives appear to have
been space and security—that security which has eluded them
despite scores of military victories.

Even today, nearly twelve years later, a smokescreen of war
propaganda and secrecy fudges the details of the operation.
(A retired French air general told me recently, with a smile,
that histories of the event still cast doubt on whether French
squadrons struck at Egypt from Israeli bases. They did.) But

* The French establishment was sure that the fall of Nasser would extinguish
the Algerian rebellion just as the Washington establishment thought that the
destruction of Hanoi would extinguish the Vietcong.

the main outlines are clear enough. By preagreement, the Israelis attacked on October 29, their planes catching the Egyptians, as always, unprepared, and the Israeli armor charging through the Sinai toward the canal. The next day, London and Paris issued an ultimatum to both combatants ordering them to pull back from the Suez Canal so that the British and French forces could occupy it. The Israelis, of course, accepted the ultimatum, and the Egyptians, of course, rejected it. All according to plan.

On the third day, British and French planes joined the attack on Egyptian airfields. Meanwhile, the Anglo-French landing forces were being assembled, with a sluggishness that must have exasperated the Israeli commander, Moshe Dayan. While the United Nations called vainly on the three allies to withdraw, the United States and the Soviet Union discovered a rare harmony of interest. It is debatable which was more effective, Moscow's nuclear threat or Washington's warning of withdrawal of financial support for the pound. In any event, Eden caved in, and then the French threw up their hands. Not so the Israelis. They halted only after occupying all of the Sinai and announcing the annexation of the Gaza Strip. They withdrew, four months later, only after the United States had virtually promised that it would keep the Gulf of Aqaba open to Israeli ships, by force, if necessary. This was a net gain for Israel, which before 1956 had to import all her oil through Haifa. By the next big crisis, Aqaba could be called Israel's "lifeline."

II

If history does not repeat itself, it often conveys the sensation of *déjà vu*. In both the Suez show and the 1967 affair, the immediate political issue, at least for Western opinion, was freedom of navigation. But in both cases there had been a prior rise of tension on the Israeli-Syrian border. Now forgotten in the dreary annals of border troubles in the Holy Land is the punitive attack by Israel on Syria in the winter of 1955–56 and the resolution introduced by the United States, Britain, and France in the United Nations Security Council and unanimously adopted, condemning that attack as a "flagrant violation" of the armistice. In April, 1967, there again was heavy fighting on the Syrian border. It is vain to try to sort out who started it; every Israeli border incident was preceded by a "provocation" from the other side. This one, however, had a sequel more serious than a U.N. resolution. Cairo, stung by criticism that it had stood idly by when Syria was attacked, sent its military chiefs to Damascus for talks.

Moscow is said to have warned its Arab friends that Israel was massing for an all-out assault to crush Syria. The Israelis indignantly deny this, and say they invited the Soviet ambassador to visit the frontier himself and make sure. He wouldn't play. But the Israeli chief of staff, Gen. Itzhak Rabin, had declared as late as May 12 that the only way to end the border raids of the Arab *fedayin* was to topple the government of Syria. It was, he said later, a "simple observation of common sense." Whether it was Rabin or the Kremlin that got Nasser's wind up, the Egyptian reaction was a disaster.

While Damascus warned the United Nations that Israel was preparing a "new Suez," Nasser sent two divisions into the Sinai. On May 17, he ordered the U.N. force of truce observers to quit Egyptian soil. U Thant promptly yielded. (To the storm of criticism that beat upon him, he replied that legally he could do nothing else. His little force was there only by consent of the Egyptians, who noted that the Israelis had never allowed the U.N. troops on *their* side of the border.) Emboldened, Nasser declared the Gulf of Aqaba closed to Israeli ships and any others bearing "strategic" cargo for Elath. With this hollow gesture (it developed later that he did not even fortify his position at the mouth of the gulf), the world was confronted with a dreadful specter: the destruction of Israel, either by economic strangulation or by the assault of 100 million Arabs.

It was of course a fraudulent specter, and it did not frighten the Israeli general staff. "I do not think Nasser wanted war," General Rabin said in a remarkable interview in *Le Monde* on February 29, 1968. "The two divisions he sent into the Sinai on May 14 would not have been enough to launch an offensive against Israel. He knew it, and we knew it." But the world did not know it.

The reaction of the major capitals was prompt and varied, if not effectual. In Washington, President Johnson called upon Cairo to abandon its "illegal" blockade,* and moved rather half-heartedly toward a joint effort by the maritime powers to break it. But nobody believed that the United States, bogged down in Vietnam and concerned about its stake in Mideast oil, would risk a military confrontation over Aqaba. Moscow, apparently taken off guard by Nasser's ebullience, publicly defended the Arab case but privately appealed to President Johnson to join it in urging both sides to hold their fire. Bonn showed its concern by flying 25,000 gas masks to Israel.

In Paris, President de Gaulle refused to join an Allied attack, verbal or otherwise, on the Gulf of Aqaba. Instead,

---

* Whether the closing of the three-mile-wide strait was illegal is debatable, but there is little question that it was wrong.

he called for a joint effort by the United States, the Soviet Union, Britain, and France to preserve peace. From hindsight —which is the only good vantage point for judging de Gaulle's more shocking initiatives—this seems to have been the best hope there was. Unfortunately, although Washington agreed, Moscow turned him down. (The crisis was an awkward affair for the Kremlin, torn between Arab intransigence and its knowledge of Arab weakness.) De Gaulle did not even get credit for a good try; the most sober newspaper in the United States commented, with gloomy satisfaction, "Even President de Gaulle, who is apparently willing to throw Israel to the sharks . . . has been rebuffed in his effort to achieve a four-power conference." But de Gaulle did not stop at what some critics took as a grandstand play. That same day, May 24, he received Foreign Minister Abba Eban and, according to Israeli sources, gave him a most undiplomatic dressing down. De Gaulle seems to have been persuaded that the Israelis were contemplating war; given the long and intimate relationship of the French and Israeli secret services, he may have known it. De Gaulle himself described the interview—or monologue, as he presented it—in his celebrated November 27 press conference:

If Israel is attacked, I told him then in substance, we will not let you be destroyed, but if you attack, we will condemn your undertaking. Certainly, despite the numerical inferiority of your population, considering that you are much better organized, much more unified, much better armed than the Arabs, I do not doubt that if it comes to that you would obtain military success. But then you would find yourselves engaged in growing difficulties, on the ground and from the international point of view, all the more in that the war in the Far East cannot fail to spread a deplorable tension in the world and to have very unfortunate consequences in many countries—so much so that they will little by little put the blame on you, as conquerors.*

Eban confirmed the essentials of this account. He denied that de Gaulle had promised on May 24 that he would defend Israel, but he conceded that "this position was expressed by the general on several other occasions" and possibly "during the two weeks that preceded the six-day war."

"I had the impression that he feared a great catastrophe," Eban said, "and I gathered that he feared the outbreak of a world war. He repeated with great agitation, 'Don't make war.' I think I had much more reason than him to be nervous, but I was not."

However cool Mr. Eban may have been, the Israeli cabinet is reported to have been closely divided, through that final week, over whether to attack or not. As late as May 29, Prime Minister Eshkol told the Knesset that "practical consultations" on reopening the Gulf of Aqaba were under way, and "Israel is deeply impressed by the unambiguous stand of the United States." It may well be that the die was cast only the following day, when Nasser and King Hussein of Jordan signed a mutual-defense pact. This challenged the fundamentals of Israel's strategy, as frankly explained by Eban only ten weeks before, in a news conference reported by *The Times* of London: "Diversity and pluralism are the natural conditions of the Middle East. Israel's hope and doctrine are that the Middle East can remain a mosaic, not a monolith." Despite the perpetual troubles on the Jordanian border, the

---

* De Gaulle's insistence on associating the Vietnamese war with the trouble in the Middle East was a frequent irritant to Washington. Yet it seems evident that the Vietnam commitment virtually paralyzed American initiative in the Arab-Israeli crisis, and hardly encouraged the Soviet Union to move toward a detente. The United Nations, too, was demoralized by its helplessness in Vietnam.

Israelis had always regarded Hussein as their greatest asset in the Arab world; his brief flirtation with his militant neighbors ("Israel Encircled," said the headline in *Le Monde*) may have seemed to the Israelis to call for desperate measures. On June 1, General Dayan, the hero of Suez and a well-known hawk, was called back as Defense Minister. Although France now publicly warned that it would brand the first to open fire as an aggressor, and followed this by declaring an arms embargo—and although the United States announced that an Egyptian vice president was on his way to Washington, presumably to negotiate a settlement—it was too late.

(In the interview with *Le Monde* cited above, General Rabin was asked why Israel had attacked when it knew that Nasser was ready to yield on Aqaba, which in any case was not a life-and-death issue for Israel. He replied, "The closing of the gulf of Aqaba was in itself a *casus belli* [grounds for war] to us. However, fundamentally, the war was provoked by an ensemble of factors of a local and international nature. The nefarious role of the Soviet Union came to exacerbate the passions and hatred reigning in the area." The trouble, he said, could only finally be uprooted by a definitive peace, but this, he added, did not mean the restoration of all of the occupied territories. "The Arabs must understand," he explained, "that one does not provoke wars with impunity. This one, like the previous ones, will have to cost them something." In Israel, General Rabin is regarded as a dove.)

The six-day war needs no recounting here. It followed the course that had been predicted by military intelligence in Washington, Paris, and no doubt Moscow. It was only the Western public that had feared a different outcome. After it was all over, sensitive observers might well have wondered whether, in light of the overwhelming Israeli victory, the danger had indeed been so great as to justify a preventive war, and whether, in the light of the territorial claims immediately announced by Dayan and others, justice was indeed all on one side. But if anybody who shaped public opinion during the crisis has since publicly retracted, it has not come to my attention, although it was ironic to read the following, ten months after the war, in that great liberal newspaper *Le Monde:*

Terrorism, border incidents, repeated warnings, reprisal raids, cease-fires painfully negotiated while awaiting new battles: one might think oneself carried back a year. . . . It suffices to say that, as it was easy to foresee, the victory of last June has resolved nothing.

It was not so easy to foresee in June. *Le Monde* had editorially prayed for peace, but its Tel Aviv and United Nations correspondents were openly partisan, and its guest writers filled its columns with appeals for beleaguered Israel and denunciations of French neutrality. It was only well after the Israeli victory was assured that the views of a few intellectuals friendly to the Arabs began to appear. The rest of the press was more hawkish; only the Communist *L'Humanité* sided with the Arabs, and this only at the cost of outcries and resignations among the party faithful. A poll found that only 6 percent of Frenchmen thought the Israelis were responsible for the war—and most of these declined to go so far as to say they sympathized with the Arabs.

The Gaullist ranks also were seriously split. The government, with a nominal majority of one vote in the National Assembly, was taking a line that flouted the deep emotions of a substantial number of its deputies, three of whom flew to Israel on a solidarity mission. They returned openly critical of their government. It was just as well for the regime that the

Assembly was not in session, although there is nothing in de Gaulle's record to suggest that he would have behaved differently. The opposition, naturally, charged to the attack. For Guy Mollet, it was the justification of Suez. De Gaulle, he said, was a Pontius Pilate, and if other countries were to follow his example in washing their hands of the affair, "what a monstrous pogrom!" Nobody but the Communists agreed with the regime, and they would not admit they were doing so.

The government's June 2 warning that it would condemn the side that opened fire was greeted with derision and disbelief; when it carried out its word, it was greeted with shock and outrage. (Nobody seems to have recalled John Foster Dulles' warning on November 10, 1955, that the United States "will be strongly opposed to the side which starts a war in the Middle East, and very favorably disposed to the side which convinces the United States that it desires to maintain the peace.")

De Gaulle's arms embargo was another target of anguished complaints; for many people, the myth of an Israel in dire peril survived even the destruction of her enemies. (What price victory now?) A chorus of warnings appeared that, as a well-known journalist wrote, "the career of France as a military supplier is compromised." It was said that nobody would buy French weapons if supplies were going to be cut off in an emergency. This was a frivolous and cynical argument, which collapsed when other foreign countries did place orders for French jets, tanks, and rockets.

The arms embargo was, in fact, a rather shady affair, which seems to have been mounted chiefly to bemuse Arab opinion. There was no formal proclamation, and reporters never were able to learn its terms, if any. At first, officials assured us that it was total, and they flatly denied persistent rumors of arms shipments to Israel by way of the Netherlands and other routes. Months later, they blandly let it be known that the embargo had never applied to parts and light weapons, but only to offensive matériel—in short, only to the fifty Mirage jets Israel had ordered long before.

France has achieved some remarkable balancing feats, such as her ability to flout the U.N. arms embargo against South Africa while keeping the friendship of her former black colonies. But she evidently decided that the Mirages previously delivered to Israel had done sufficient damage; a new delivery would have to wait until some offsetting sale to the Arab side could be announced. Above all, it would have to wait for the conclusion of delicate negotiations for Iraqi oil and sulfur, which might render France totally independent of American and British suppliers. A liberal observer might well express disgust at the whole dirty business of arms and oil, but this would come with poor grace from an American or a Briton. (The argument of French strategists is that a nation cannot have an independent foreign policy without an independent defense industry, which a relatively small country cannot maintain without export markets. On its own premises, the argument is hard to attack.) It was interesting that a contract for the sale of seventy armored cars to Iraq, signed in November, was not announced until about ten weeks later— the day after Washington announced it would furnish arms to Jordan.

### III

By the time the Assembly reconvened in the fall, Israel had ceased to be a major political issue in France. In the first place it was hard now to evoke an Arab peril. At the same time, un-easiness had begun to spread in the French left about Israel's territorial intentions, and about the all-too-familiar conse-quences of Israel's occupation of a hostile land—suspension of civil liberties, political arrests, and terror. In a letter to the press, a veteran of the French resistance objected to the term terrorist as applied to Arabs; he said the Germans had used the same word against the resistants.

On the center and right, meanwhile, the realization grew that France had not emerged too badly from the crisis, all things considered. In fact, of all countries concerned, she seemed to have done the best. Israel won a victory but not peace or security (an unidentified Arab leader has been quoted as saying, "They taught us one thing: Strike without warn-ing"). The Arabs, of course, suffered a humiliating and bloody defeat. The United States, by lining up politically with Israel, gained a deep and probably lasting enmity in the Arab world. For Britain, the war was an unmitigated disaster. The closing of the Suez Canal and the heavy withdrawal of Arab funds from London banks were a major factor in the subsequent collapse of the pound and the precarious British footing in the Arab oil sheikdoms was seriously undermined. For the Soviet Union, the balance sheet is not yet closed. It lost a lot of weapons, but is not that what weapons are for? Most Western observers happily associated Moscow with the Arabs in a common humiliation, but history may conclude that the Israeli war finally achieved an old dream of the tsars: making Russia a Mediterranean power. As for France, her gains were indisputable. Herself at war with the Arabs as recently as 1962, she was now, suddenly, the Arabs' only friend in the Western world.

For Americans and Britons, it might seem not a bad thing

to have a Western interlocutor dealing with a hostile Middle East, but "Anglo-Saxon" opinion has been in no mood to accept favors from France. I recall two cases in point, where I had occasion to learn the facts, as opposed to the versions generally presented to the public. The first involved the short-lived oil blockade imposed by the Arabs after the Israeli victory. The United States Department of the Interior hastily declared a state of emergency, because of the threat to the *European* oil supply (America being, of course, self-sufficient). This exasperated the European authorities. In the first place, they did not face an acute emergency, because they had maintained good reserve stocks since the Suez affair. More important, they saw no point in encouraging solidarity among the Arabs by vaunting the solidarity of the West. This attitude was most disappointing to an American oil rescue mission that flew to Paris for a meeting at the OECD, the economic agency of the Western powers. The Europeans declined to save face for Washington by declaring an emergency, but quiet steps were taken toward rationing oil tankers and supplies if necessary. The Americans were surprised to find, as they admitted privately, that the French were extremely co-operative, behind closed doors. At the same time, however, a minor revision of French oil import regulations was seized upon, notably by the British press, as a sign that Paris was helping the Arabs to plug leaks in the oil embargo. There was absolutely no basis to this interpretation, which was simply another sign of the irrational state of public opinion—and opinion makers. At this point, any stick would do to beat a dog. Another one came handy when, at this very moment, Paris had to notify London officially that she would not take part in the proposed joint development of a swing-wing plane. This was not really news; the French had informally advised the British months earlier, but had been asked not to make it final until the end of the period agreed upon for study of the project, which was June 30. The British press forgot that it had itself derided the swing-wing project as a costly and foolish effort to combine two different aircraft into one model, and also forgot that it was the French who were the driving force behind the Concorde and other Franco-British joint ventures. Scare headlines told the British they had been stabbed in the back again by you know who. A leading American newspaper combined the two fictitious betrayals, on oil and the swing-wing plane, into one analysis captioned "Perfidious Gaul." The dispatch described the British state of mind accurately and sympathetically, but did not make plain that it was based on fantasy.

France again was widely berated when Iraq invited her to bid—against the Soviet Union, among others—for new oil fields. French oil men pointed out to their American and British partners in the Iraq Petroleum Company that the fields were, in any case, lost for good as far as the IPC was concerned, and they privately offered to cut the others in for a share of any oil recovered. British oil men were inclined to accept this approach, but the State Department insisted on making a stern protest to the Quai d'Orsay. It should be added that, while these difficult but promising oil negotiations were going on, de Gaulle refused to encourage the Arabs in an intransigent line toward Israel. After his meeting with President Aref of Iraq, de Gaulle's spokesman declared publicly that the two men had agreed on "some" points regarding Israel, but had *disagreed* on others.

By fall, then, Gaullists were able to argue persuasively that everything the general had done had been in the interest of France and in the interest of peace—and thus in the interest of the whole world. But any forgiveness he might have earned among liberals was dissipated by one deplorable passage of his November 27 press conference.

## IV

It was no slip of the tongue. De Gaulle prepares his rare press conferences with great care, and this was a jewel. The general was good-humored and alert, and took evident zest in sending the crockery flying in all directions. He twitted the press, waxed ironic on his own mortality, and in his own lofty historic style lectured the United States, Britain, Canada, and Israel. The damage was done in a few sentences—a few words, rather—of his discourse on Israel. The context has not, so far as I know, received general publication abroad. Here it is:

The establishment between the two world wars—for one must indeed go back that far—of a Zionist home in Palestine and, following the second world war, the establishment of a State of Israel, gave rise at the time to a certain number of apprehensions. One could indeed ask oneself, and one asked oneself even among many Jews, whether the implantation of that community, on land acquired under more or less justifiable conditions and in the midst of Arab peoples fundamentally hostile, would not bring incessant, interminable frictions and conflicts. And some even feared that the Jews, until then dispersed, who had remained what they had been forever—that is an elite people, sure of itself and *dominateur* —might not once reassembled come to turn into ardent and conquering ambition the very moving wishes they had expressed for nineteen centuries: "next year in Jerusalem."

In spite of the sometimes rising, sometimes falling tide of malevolence which they induced—more exactly, which they gave rise to—in certain countries at certain periods, a considerable capital of interest and even sympathy had built up in their favor and especially, it must be said, within Christianity. A capital growing out of the immense repository of the Testament, nourished from all the sources of a magnificent liturgy, sustained by the commiseration that their age-old tragedy inspired and which among us entered poetry with the legend of the "wandering Jew," enhanced by the abominable persecutions they had suffered during the Second World War and enlarged since they had found again a homeland by their constructive work and the courage of their soldiers. That is why, independently of the vast support in money, in influence, in propaganda that the Israelis received from Jewish circles in America and Europe, many countries, France among them, viewed with satisfaction the establishment of their state on what the powers recognized as its territory, while still wishing it could, by using some modesty, find a peaceful modus vivendi with its neighbors. . . .

Alas, the tragedy arrived.

In the phrase that received the most attention, "an elite people, sure of itself and *dominateur*," the last word was nearly everywhere rendered as "domineering." This is not unfair to de Gaulle, since he must be held responsible for what his words *may* imply. Just for the record, however, French dictionaries give as the first meaning of *dominateur* the literal notion of conquering or ruling, best translated as "dominating." "Wanting to dominate"—that is, domineering —comes second. The antonyms, or opposites, of *dominateur*, incidentally, are given as "humble, oppressed, submissive."

Whether he meant dominating or domineering or both, the extraordinary thing is that de Gaulle meant it as a compliment! He was about to deliver a tongue-lashing to the Jewish state (as he did to the American, British, and Canadian states) and to declare formally ended that special relationship between France and Israel exemplified by the Suez affair. He chose to soften this harsh message with one of the finest things he could say about any nation. Had not his life's work, since the French debacle of 1940, been to persuade his own countrymen that they were *un peuple d'élite, sûr de lui-même et dominateur?* In the event, the political scolding was generally ignored; it was the flattery that inflicted the pain. The reaction of many Jews was crystallized in one brilliant, terrible drawing by Tim, the only editorial cartoon ever published by *Le Monde.* It showed a skeletal Jew behind the barbed wire of a concentration camp; the caption: "*Sûr de Lui-Même et Dominateur.*"

Leaders of the Jewish community in France, very likely for the first time in its history, publicly rebuked the chief of state. In a declaration criticized by some as too mild, Chief Rabbi Jacob Kaplan suggested that the president might be "giving the highest possible sanction to a campaign of discrimination."

Abroad, critics accused de Gaulle of blatant antisemitism. This charge did not make much headway in France, where the study of de Gaulle is almost a separate historic discipline. Critics acknowledged that no trace of prejudice could be found in his career, which is remarkable, considering his background—the military-bourgeois caste that in his childhood shook the republic over the Dreyfus affair. (Perhaps even more remarkable is that his family is said to have taken the side of the Jewish Captain Dreyfus, a position then regarded as treasonable to church and state. It should be mentioned in passing that a majority of the French people finally swung behind Dreyfus, and brought into power a liberal, anticlerical party, the Radical Socialists, which governed for half a century.)

Writers recalled that there had always been men of Jewish descent among de Gaulle's close collaborators, from the wartime resistance movement to his present cabinet. But this counting of heads was only another ugly consequence of de Gaulle's unfortunate remarks. If condescension toward victims of prejudice ("Some of my best friends are Jews"; "I think you Negroes have a marvelous sense of rhythm") has lately been banned from polite society, then surely a statesman has no business describing a people, including many of his own citizens, in terms of national traits. In criticizing de Gaulle, however, a difficulty immediately arose: the objectionable implication that the Jews were a people apart was a fundamental premise of Zionism. This was promptly recognized by that doughty, certainly *dominateur* old warrior Ben-Gurion. In a public statement and in a letter to de Gaulle, he warmly defended his country and its behavior and termed some of the general's comments as "wounding," but deplored "the unjust criticism formulated by many people in France, in Israel, and in other countries who, I think, have not examined your observations with all the attention needed." He repeated, as he had maintained for more than half a century, that Palestine—all of Palestine—had "never been the sole and unique fatherland of any other people than the Jewish people," and that the Arabs had plenty of territory, while the Jews, prior to Zionism, had none.

"We are a small people," Ben-Gurion told de Gaulle, "a majority of whom do not live in their country." "I know," he said, "that for hundreds of years the Christian world was convinced that the Jewish people had ceased to exist two thousand years ago, and I know also that there are Jews who think the same way; we pitied these Jews, but we are not angry with them—they want to stop being Jews, that's their personal affair." Ben-Gurion had long ago said the same thing, bluntly, to American Jews; in effect, they were Israelis or not Jews at all. There were no exceptions to the ingathering of Jewry; the new state needed more land for security in a hostile Arab world, and more people to occupy the land. It was not money but pioneers that would reestablish Zion.* This posed a painful dilemma for the Jews of such countries as France, Britain, and the United States, who regard *those* countries as their homelands and are accepted as such. Most of them had rejected Zionism on that ground, until the Nazi holocaust. They had every right of course to lend support to Israel —and the Jews were not alone in that—but they risked being accused of putting the interest of a foreign country above that of their own. So a number of Jews in France took public issue with Edmond de Rothschild, who in a circular appealing for—or, rather, demanding—funds had declared. "The military victory of Israel was a victory of the Jewish people, isolated in a hostile or indifferent world," and added, "The contribution required from each of us does not constitute an act of charity, it's a tax, it's the price of our dignity, of our pride, of our solidarity." Similar protests greeted the declaration of Daniel Mayer, former head of the the French Socialist Party, at the height of the June fever: "I am ashamed of being a Frenchman, since the official policy of France, for the second time in less than thirty years, means the abandonment in the hour of danger of a friendly and allied country. I am ashamed of being a human being, since nothing is being done by humanity against the repetition of genocide. In order to reply to some in advance, I add that I am not ashamed of

* After each Israeli victory has come an appeal for massive immigration. Premier Eshkol issued one on October 28, 1967, pointing out that only 64 percent of the population of "greater Israel" was now Jewish. Jews evicted from Arab countries have formed the bulk of immigration since 1948, but these communities, which had lived in the Arab world for thousands of years, have virtually ceased to exist. Many of the refugees, incidentally, preferred to settle in France, which also has quietly helped the last survivors in Arab countries to get out.

being Jewish." In the streets, young marchers, mostly Jewish, were shouting, *"La France avec nous!"* A student was overheard demanding of a Jewish classmate, "France on *our* side? Why don't you holler, 'France on *their* side'?" The excesses of Jewish fervor can be written off to the fears and passions of the moment, like the accompanying movement of a few New York garment manufacturers for a boycott of their French competitors. One may hope that, given the liberal traditions of France, these incitements to antisemitism will fall on barren soil.

General de Gaulle, who had less excuse than the Jews to be carried away, came probably as close to apologizing as his character would permit. In a reply to Ben-Gurion, he repeated the essence of his November 27 critique of Israeli policy, but expressed surprise that "some people affect to regard as pejorative" his description of *un peuple d'élite, sûr de lui-même et dominateur*, "whereas it cannot be at all disobliging to emphasize the quality thanks to which this strong people was able to survive and remain itself after nineteen centuries passed under unheard of conditions." The Elysée Palace made public his letter, along with Ben-Gurion's. At the same time, it announced that at a New Year's reception for religious leaders, de Gaulle had taken Chief Rabbi Kaplan off for a warm chat, and had assured him that he had meant no offense. The *dominateur* affair was closed, Rabbi Kaplan said.

Not entirely, I'm afraid. "As it was easy to foresee," *Le Monde* had written, "the victory of last June has resolved nothing." Until a lasting peace is achieved in the Middle East —and it is difficult to see how Israeli claims are to be reconciled with Arab dignity—there will linger a certain awkwardness in relations among French Jews, and between French

Jews and non-Jews. As for Americans and Britons, they have too many other grievances, real or imagined, against de Gaulle to give a thoughtful reconsideration to his behavior toward Israel. Else they might conclude that, after all, except for the one lapse of judgment on November 27, his conduct had been a model for the world.

# 3

# DE GAULLE AND THE DOLLAR

> *A Boston landlord threatened publicly to make the French consul pay his rent in gold. . . . An ad in* Women's Wear Daily *warned that to buy French couture is to attack the dollar. . . . An American manufacturer canceled an order for French pipefittings on the ground that the French Government was trying "to upset and destroy the American monetary system."*

IT IS ODD THAT, of all the rich assortment of grievances against de Gaulle, some Americans should choose as the most flagrant his supposed war against the dollar. It is odd because it displays a curious sense of values; one can better understand a righteous indignation against de Gaulle for his ouster of our troops, his denunciation of our "detestable war" in Vietnam, his rudeness toward our British, Canadian, and Israeli friends. It is odd because honest, well-informed men can take either side of any of these issues except the myth that France has been waging an underhanded assault on the dollar, which has no basis in fact or common sense. It is odd because most Americans would candidly admit that they had only the foggiest knowledge of what the monetary scrap was all about.

This sort of candor is, unfortunately, a luxury generally denied to reporters. Instant expertise is our daily bread, and it would simply not do for us to announce in our coverage of space exploration, heart surgery, grain futures, or border disputes that our ignorance is only slightly less dense, if at all, than that of our readers. But it happens that the press itself has played a role, if a minor one, in the monetary follies of our time, and if we are to understand the action, we shall have to go backstage.

First, we must face the fact that financial reporting is not the strongest area of American journalism. There are good men in the field (in spite of the fact that industry is constantly luring bright ones away), but in the majority, the financial pages are staffed by people who think business news is dull and who write it that way. Where a Fabre or a Maeterlinck found a fascinating, teeming jungle, in which thousands of creatures were waging a perpetual struggle for survival, we common folk see only a peaceful meadow. Blind to the real drama unfolding in the jungle of economic life, the financial reporter is reduced to creating a synthetic drama: "Market Tries to Rally but Fails." This is pure anthropomorphism, a return to primitive superstition. The market is of course not a person, but a meeting place of buyer and seller (who are of course the same people, at different times), each doing what self-interest seems to dictate. They are trying to *anticipate* the market, not push it in one direction or another; the fables of bulls and bears, and of speculators "mounting an attack on the pound" are fantasy, promoted by poor reporters and, on occasion, by politicians. "Panics" and "frenzied markets" are nearly always more or less pure journalistic fiction. In "panics" such as the recent runs on sterling and the recent gold rushes, who was being panicky, the buyer or the seller? Newsmen would be well advised to await the verdict of history.

It may be asked how newsmen get away with bad reporting among people, such as businessmen, who know the facts. An easy answer is that we have the only wheel in town, but the truth is more intriguing. A banker was asked some years ago what he thought of a certain financial news section; he replied that it was excellent—sober, well informed, intelligent—except in banking, where it did not know its proverbial from its proverbial. Experts hardly ever trust the press in their own fields, but their own fields are limited. In the land of the blind, the one-eyed man is king.

Who were, in fact, the speculators who attacked the pound? An indication may be found in the embarrassment that struck the First National City Bank of New York in the spring of 1965. A bright young reporter (he's working for a bank himself now) noticed a small item in a prospectus, revealing that National City had lost $7.5 million in foreign-exchange dealings. A little digging uncovered the fact that, at a time when the Federal Reserve was pouring out huge sums to support the pound, National City was selling pounds short, to the tune of somewhere upward of $500 million. It explained that this was the doing of an overzealous employee in Brussels. The affair was soon forgotten, as well it might be, for nobody would, or should, accuse National City of mounting a deliberate attack on the pound. On the contrary nobody has, to my knowledge, criticized American banks and other corporations—or British banks, for that matter—for having unloaded even larger amounts of sterling during the major crises that have hit the pound (and the dollar behind it). *The New York Times* reported after the devaluation of November, 1967, that none of the American companies in Britain would admit having lost anything, and some may even have earned a profit. This implied that in the days preceding the event they had transferred hundreds of millions of dollars' worth of pounds into other currencies, thus helping to precipitate the devaluation and forcing the Allied monetary authorities to spend that many more dollars to keep the market orderly while they were trying to make up their minds. No criticism of the American companies is intended or implied; if they had behaved otherwise and lost money in sterling, their stockholders would have fair grounds to accuse management of imprudence. (That weekend, a few American banks and corporations did in fact get caught with sterling, but they did not boast about it to the *Times*.) British banks also, it should be pointed out, heeded the dictates of prudence, as did all well-advised large holders of funds. The chief direct victims of devaluation were small British depositors and those Arab oil sheiks who had permitted high British interest rates to overcome their political prejudices.

So the "speculators mounting an attack on the pound" were, in large part, prudent American and British corporations, rather than the "gnomes of Zurich" assailed by Harold Wilson. (The Swiss bankers quite often act as agents for British and American accounts, which incidentally helps to explain why British yachts choke the harbors of the Côte d'Azur whose owners may not legally spend more than £50 a year abroad.)

Now, what may be forgiven of private business may not be pardoned of public authorities. But in all the "raids" on the pound and dollar *the Bank of France played no part*. From the summer of 1966 to spring of 1968, when these lines were being written, the bank added not an ounce of gold to its hoard. In fact, during the gold rush of November–December, 1967, when more than $420 million of scared money was transferred from British to French banks, France quietly suspended her policy of turning her surplus foreign exchange into gold. At the same time, she contributed $230 million toward an International Monetary Fund credit of $1.5 billion to support the pound, and renewed a separate loan of $100 million to Britain. She acted, as did other Western governments, not out of charity nor a desire to maintain the present monetary system unchanged, but out of fear that a collapse of the pound and the dollar could lead to a panic that would shake the economies of the whole world.

Yet the notion persists in a large segment of American opinion, and an even larger segment of British opinion, that it was de Gaulle who mounted the attack on the dollar and the pound. This delusion is based on a dim awareness that his government has been a bitter critic of the existing international monetary system; its frequent warnings that it could lead only to a crash have been taken to imply that France *wanted* a crash and would do what it could to bring it about. This idea has been actively propagated by American officials, one of whom publicly accused France of "mischief-making" in the gold rush of late 1967. More often, the blame is spread in "backgrounders," which are sessions in which public officials give selected reporters information, on condition that the sources are not identified. A typical result of a backgrounder is the following dispatch to *The Guardian* of London during the gold rush of March, 1968:

There seems little doubt in American minds that France has done everything to aggravate and exploit U.S. and British balance of payment difficulties. Some profess to believe that General de Gaulle has done this as part of his effort to force the U.S. to make peace in Vietnam (the war is a major cause of the U.S. balance of payments deficit), but others attribute it more simply to a French desire to humiliate Britain and the U.S.

The dispatch came from Paris, not Washington, and *The Guardian's* correspondent could only have learned what was going on in "American minds" (meaning Washington minds) from an American official. Among those who were in Paris that week were the chief White House economic adviser and an undersecretary of the Treasury, but the thinking could have come from any of a dozen others. Whoever it was, he is covered by the correspondent's code of secrecy and is at liberty to deny he ever said any such thing. Thus he can with impunity toss any number of dead cats at his host country; he can assiduously spread the idea—which he may half believe—that it is French perfidy and not any shortcomings of American or British policy making that is responsible for the trouble we are in. And he can even accuse other people of mischief-making.

To succeed, this kind of bushwhacking needs special cooperation from the press. Responsible papers do not normally repeat anonymous accusations, nor do they publish even open accusations without trying to give the other side. But where France is concerned, fair play and even common sense do not apply. When the French Finance Minister talked, on the record, to an international mob of newsmen at Stockholm, the usually sophisticated *Economist* said, "M. Debré held several conspiratorial briefings in the hotel lounge." Another reporter seems to have had a really conspiratorial chat with an American official concerning the secret meeting of central bankers in Washington in mid-March, 1968. He wrote what the official, identified as "sources close to the negotiations" and "informed observers," was willing to reveal about the secret decisions (actually, it was a rather dubious and self-serving "scoop"). Then he went on, "The French had been excluded from the Washington talks, it was said, because of the consistent pattern that has developed in recent months of information 'leaks' from the French Treasury to the Paris newspaper *Le Monde*. Time after time, these sources asserted, the most 'perverse and disruptive interpretations possible' of private and confidential conversations between governments had been promptly reported in *Le Monde*." This is an exaggerated version of a charge I will discuss further on. I mention it here merely to indicate the state of mind that views the betrayal of secrets as naughty only when the other chap does it.

Yet with all the eager help of our bemused journalists, the myth that France is to blame for our monetary crises could never have flourished were it not for the wall of ignorance that keeps truly expert opinion from the public. For a great majority of economists and bankers, in the United States and Britain as elsewhere, have long agreed that the monetary ship was taking water and would need a major overhaul to stay afloat. Such warnings, unfortunately in language impenetrable to the layman, are standard features of such arcane publications as *The Wall Street Journal*, the *Financial Times* of London, and the monthly letters of leading banks. They draw snickers, to be sure, from young men raking in the chips in this best of all possible worlds, secure in the knowledge that the dollar is better than gold. The rest of the world, unfortunately, has not felt all that secure. In the last few years I have talked about money to scores of European businessmen, international bankers, and financial writers, and have found not one—I repeat, not one—who was not critical of the prevailing system. Their criticism may be summarized as follows:

Paper money is a good, even indispensable, way of handling international business. Country A buys something in Country B and pays with an IOU called currency. Country B spends it in Country C, and it circulates around until it gets home. The books finally balance. No country can long spend more than it earns (in technical terms, run a payments deficit), else other countries will stop accepting its IOU's at face value. But the wheel is rigged in favor of the so-called reserve currency countries—the United States and Britain. Dollars and pounds are used by other countries not merely to spend but also as a reserve depository and backing for their own currencies—the role once held exclusively by gold. As a result, the United States and Britain can print and spend *more* IOU's than they earn from the rest of the world. And this we have done with a will, to the tune of billions and billions of dollars. When other countries run their printing presses overtime, the laws of economics call them to account: Prices rise, governments fall, belts are tightened. But the United States and Britain can, as the saying goes, "export their inflation." And so we have created and spent billions and billions of dollars more than we have earned, and fired them into orbit. The Europeans argue that the ability to buy something for nothing gives the "Anglo-Saxons" an unfair advantage; they complain that we are buying their industry with their own money. Lately they have added, with some justice, that they were being forced to finance the Vietnamese war as well.

"Anglo-Saxons" often argue that foreigners are better off with dollars and pounds than with gold; paper can be "put to work," while gold cannot. I'm afraid this is another of those cases where a discussion is clouded by anthropomorphism, which gives a living personality to an inanimate thing. Money does not work, period. As an accepted token of value, it can be lent out, at interest—whether it is paper, metal, or seashells. Gold has of course been lent out since the beginning of time, either physically or in the form of paper notes, just as checks are written to represent dollars that are presumed to be in the bank. (In fact, we only pretend that the dollars are there. Banks are required to keep just one dollar in reserve for every six in their checking accounts. The system works very well.) It is true that central banks earn nothing on their bullion, while they generally draw interest on their dollar and pound reserves, which they invest in Treasury bills in London or New York. Europeans look on this as a mixed blessing. First, they point out that this system, in which the Anglo-Saxons print IOU's, spend them in Europe, and borrow them back at low interest rates, allows them to spend the same money twice. Further, they argue that this system is a good source of funds for the United States and Britain only if they have a sound, productive use for it. The cost of paying interest on foreigners' money was one of the burdens that brought down the pound.

The Europeans admit, to be sure, that the system was extremely useful in providing funds to impoverished Europe just after the war (which is not to say that some better system might not have been devised). But the assumption that made it work was that, in the long run, the Anglo-Saxons would honor their IOU's—that is, that they would stop spending more than they were earning abroad. Otherwise, worldwide inflation would grow, people would lose confidence in money, and a bust would be inevitable. There was a safety valve built into the system: The United States stood ready to pay out gold for its IOU's, at $35 an ounce, to any foreign country that asked for it. In theory, a continuing deficit would thus finally call us to account. This was the famous Gold Exchange Standard. I use the past tense deliberately. When the United States gold supply fell to the danger level, the government did not take the orthodox measure of halting the payments deficit— it simply tied down the safety valve. It made known to other countries that, while the gold window at the "Fed" in New York was still open for business, any effort to convert dollars would be regarded as an unfriendly act, fraught with the direst consequences for the whole world. At the same time, Federal officials began shuffling paper in a manner so complex as to baffle any but specialists in the field; they invented devices called swaps, Roosa bonds, and Special Drawing Rights, all really being disguised borrowings of foreign funds, designed to persuade the world to continue accepting dollars while the United States continued to run a payments deficit.

Washington did make sporadic efforts to reduce the deficit, but these were more than offset by the Vietnamese war and by political pressures at home. Given a sufficient sense of urgency, something might have been done long ago, but it was difficult to quarrel with the economic success of the post-war years. Prosperity induced a comfortable lethargy. We were like the indolent farmer who wouldn't fix the barn roof because he did not like to work in the rain, and it did not leak in dry weather. This logic is particularly applicable to economic policy making. A crisis is no time to talk coolly about long-range cures. During the 1967 run on the pound, for example, the British had to deny to the last minute that they would ever devalue; otherwise, the run would have cleaned out every penny in the cashbox. But as soon as the crisis let up, political pressures built up against anything like a fundamental monetary reform.

Now a great majority of the world's monetary experts, with the possible exception of those employed by the United States and British Governments,* have long agreed that such a

---

* It may well be asked why, even during moments of relative calm, experts in the government do not talk the same way as experts outside the government. The answer is that the professor turned statesman soon learns the rules of the game. When President Kennedy named Prof. Stanley Surrey, a noted critic of the income-tax law, as the Treasury's tax policy chief, a shiver went through Wall Street. Surrey did make one effort at reform, sweetened by a tax cut. Congress passed the cut, but not the reform, and Assistant Secretary Surrey went on to support precisely the kinds of policy that Professor Surrey had assailed with scorn.

reform was overdue. They agree that the gold-exchange standard was unfair and dangerous, that the day of reckoning has arrived, and that it should be replaced by a truly international, rather than dollar-based, system of money. The trouble is that they cannot agree on what system to adopt.

Lord knows that there is no lack of meritorious schemes, such as Mendès-France's idea of a money pegged to reserves of grain, sugar, and other commodities, which would be helpful to the underdeveloped countries. But nearly all the proposals put forward would require a revolution in the world's money management, following a long, painful international negotiation. There is some question as to whether we have that much time. Thus the most alluring idea to many people is the quickest and the simplest one—a return to a modified version of the gold standard. Actually, the world has never altogether left it, as witnessed by the periodic scramble for gold whenever the public loses confidence in major currencies. Gold is neutral; it has no nationality, and it is highly acceptable everywhere but in the United States, where it is regarded as sinful (in contrast with the dollar, which is productive).

A return to the gold standard has certain demerits, however, not the least being that it would tickle de Gaulle. A stronger argument is that there simply is not enough gold to meet the money needs of a growing world economy. The gold advocates reply that there would be lots more around if the United States had not frozen the price of gold in 1934 at $35 an ounce; while everything else was rising in price over the years, gold stood still. (Effectively, the dollar, pegged to gold, was being devalued constantly in terms of buying power.) Residents of the Rocky Mountain states are well aware that, if the price of gold were permitted to rise in line with other metals, hundreds of abandoned mines would reopen, and the supply of gold would grow rapidly. At the same

time, existing stocks of gold would stretch farther. Prof.
Jacques Rueff, who is credited with being de Gaulle's mentor
on the question, has suggested that doubling the price of gold
would be about right, though he does not insist on that figure.
In that case, the gold in Fort Knox would be worth $20 bil-
lion instead of $10 billion. The critics, who say there is not
enough gold at present, hereupon reverse their field and argue
that this would be inflationary. The gold advocates reply that
experts should get together and decide what price would *not*
be inflationary, or that gold should be allowed to find its own
price, according to the world's need for money, or that some
of the surplus values created by an increase in the price of
gold should be assigned by the major central banks to a fund
to help the poorer countries.

Still another objection is that a rise in the price of gold
would help not only the United States but such undeserving
countries as France, the Soviet Union, and South Africa, and
also would reward those gold hoarders who have created all
this trouble. ("My advice," Congressman Reuss told them, "is
that crime does not pay. You had better get rid of what gold
you have.") This objection falls in the realm of emotion, along
with the notion that gold is inherently evil, and is hardly subject to discussion.

There is more to both sides of this argument, which enters
the vital but difficult question of how to achieve a stability
of international exchange rates. We may here leave the debate to the experts, but I think a layman may draw this conclusion: *that the gold standard is a reasonable proposal for
discussion, and that it is not inherently anti-American or necessarily against the interests of the United States.*

But a reasonable discussion we have never had. Instead, we
have had a stubborn insistence, in the face of disaster, that

the existing system was the best that man could devise, and that the troubles besetting it were all the doing of a sinister band of gold-buying plotters, incited by that man in the Elysée Palace. During the gold rush of March, 1968, I asked one of Washington's highest policy makers at a backgrounder how the United States would meet the threat; he replied that we would hold fast. "This is a game of chicken," he said, "and we're not chicken."

The metaphor is a chilling one. The last person in the world I would want to play chicken against is a French motorist. But on the record, I do not think it can be shown that France was trying to shove the dollar into the ditch, at the risk of a general pileup. The charge of recklessness can easily be made in the opposite direction. Years ago, France began preaching, loud and clear, that the system was heading for a fall. At meetings of the International Monetary Fund and World Bank, for example, she complained that their resources, originally put together to help the poor countries, were being used to prop up two rich ones, the United States and Britain. She opposed new devices that would encourage the Anglo-Saxons to persist in their payments deficits. She demanded that the Fund apply to the Anglo-Saxons the same rules she applied to other borrowers. While other European governments found it more prudent, because of political and economic pressures, to muffle their criticism, France put her money where her mouth was. When the dollars were flowing in (this was before 1967), she presented them at the gold window of the Fed—in accordance with the rules of the game as established by the United States. And when in spite of everything the Anglo-Saxon deficits grew, she resisted throwing good money after bad to save what she regarded as a doomed system.

All this was tough behavior, but it was in the rules of the game, and a strong case can be made that it was in the best interest of all players. (If Washington and London had gone along, it is conceivable that they would have avoided several crises, and it is certain that they would have saved billions in gold.) There were charges of foul play on both sides, but I know of only two specific ones leveled against France, and neither would stand up in court. One was that she incited Algeria to buy $150 million of gold from the Fed in late 1967; there is of course no evidence that she did, and in fact none of the other countries in the franc bloc bought gold. Algeria needed no encouragement to take action against the United States, if that was the idea. The second low blow imputed to France is a more interesting affair. It involves, oddly enough, the financial reporting of *Le Monde*, the great liberal Paris newspaper, which is generally critical of de Gaulle.

There were actually three major news items that stimulated the run on sterling and the scramble for gold in November–December, 1967. None of them *caused* the break (it is an infantile notion that newspaper talk by itself can sustain a market upheaval), but they all made their mark. The first was the flight of Frederick Deming, the United States Under Secretary of the Treasury, to Basel, where the clearinghouse known as the Bank for International Settlements met on November 12. Deming had no normal business being there, and the financial world quickly and correctly concluded that something big was up. After secret talks, Deming and the central bankers adjourned without issuing a statement. Smart holders of money hastily began pulling out of sterling. Deming's flight has been described as perhaps the most costly in history. (It is curious that, in the next crisis, William McChesney Martin, chairman of the Federal Reserve Board, also flew to Basel, saying he just wanted to shoot the breeze with his European colleagues. The effect on the public was about the same as the Deming voyage.) The second big news event came three days later when the secrecy around the Deming trip was broken by, of all things, the BBC. It said Britain had asked for loans totaling $1 billion (it was more, actually) to save the pound. This meant real trouble, especially since there was no certainty that the other countries would come through, and the smart money now was sure that devaluation was imminent. It was indeed, but while the British Government was dithering over how much to devalue, and its allies were dithering over how much to lend and under what conditions, hundreds of millions of dollars had to be spent to sustain the bogus price of sterling and to meet the demand for gold. Typically, the London press meanwhile accused the French of having leaked the BBC scoop, and even a public letter of denial by the London BBC reporter responsible has not laid that canard to rest.

Devaluation came on Saturday night, and it might be noted that, while a good many countries cut their exchange rates to remain competitive with Britain, the major Western countries, including France, did not. (When a country cheapens its money, its exports become cheaper in terms of foreign currency, while imports become more expensive.) They granted Britain this edge in trade, and huge loans besides, to avoid a collapse that would overtake them all. But they were by no means out of the woods. Confidence in paper money had been badly shaken, and it did not help when Treasury Secretary Fowler declared, over the weekend, that the dollar was in the front line, now. Indeed, a massive flight into gold was now getting under way. It got a lift—it is hard to say how much— from the third big news item, which appeared in *Le Monde* that Monday afternoon. This revealed that France had stopped paying assessments to the London Gold Pool back in June.

The pool is a private club with eight members: the United States, Britain, France, West Germany, Switzerland, the Netherlands, Belgium, and Italy. Its purpose is to keep the price of gold in the free market orderly and within a narrow range of the United States price of $35 an ounce; it does this by buying gold when the price falls and selling when it rises. Until the mid-1960's, these transactions tended to balance out, with the help of Soviet gold sales. But then the world's private demand for gold began to exceed the supply of newly mined metal, and in 1967 the pool had to call on its members for more chips. The calls came $50 million at a time; after the second time, France called it quits. There were fourteen more calls from June to late November, totaling $700 million. If France had stayed in, she would have contributed, and lost, 9 percent of this, or $63 million. The United States took over her share, dropping a total of $413 million. (It is a striking fact that none of our loyal and wealthy allies offered to share the burden with us. It is even more striking that during the fall crisis, when they were supposed to be helping us meet the demand for gold, the gold reserves of Italy and Switzerland actually went up. Somebody was playing dirty pool, perhaps, but it was not France.) Now it seems good business sense, and perfectly consistent with her position, for France to have refused in June to pour out gold to support a monetary strategy she deplored. It would be harder to defend her deliberately making this fact public in November, at a time when a full-scale run on paper money was under way. But did she?

The impression that she had was strengthened by a whole series of news beats from *Le Monde*'s bright young man on the monetary beat, Paul Fabra. Other reporters often had to file dispatches reading "according to *Le Monde*," which did not make Fabra especially popular in the press corps. (It was amusing to hear Fabra blackguarded as a government mouthpiece by newsmen who make a career of "cultivating news sources" in government, and I wondered what they would have done if such scoops had been tossed in *their* laps.) It is simply not done for one reporter to ask another just where he is getting his hot news tips, but after the November crisis had subsided, I looked Fabra up and invited him to lunch, on my expense account. Over a *gigot d'agneau*, I put it to him that he had become a figure in the history of sterling devaluation, and invited him to comment, if he cared to, on the often published charge that the French Government had used him for what our Treasury was calling mischief-making. Fabra, a dark animated young man, proceeded to give an old pro an elementary lesson in financial journalism. He did not get his stories from one source, he said. Rather, he had begun by canvassing bankers and money traders in Milan, Zurich, Brussels, and London as well as Paris—"men who have the feel of the market." "By the time I was ready to approach certain people," he went on, "I already had most of the story." He did not have to say more, for it dawned upon me that, whether one accepted his account or not, the great Fabra scoop had been lying around all the time, waiting for some competent reporter to pick it up.

For several years now, the world's private demand for gold has been met by only two sources: the gold mines and the London pool. Mine production and the volume of trading in the gold market can be estimated very roughly from various sources. A reporter who followed the market could make a fairly educated guess as to the magnitude of the losses suffered by the gold pool. If he was good at statistics, he could cross-check this against the monthly figures on gold reserves of each of the member countries (with an eye also on their trade figures), and come up with an estimate of its individual loss.* This is doubtless what the best financial advisers of banking and exchange firms were doing all along, and a sophisticated reporter could have taken a shortcut by having a long chat with one of these. He could then have gone to any reasonably friendly government authority and laid the story on the line, asking only, "Am I wrong?" Another scenario would have a brash reporter telling a French official, "By my figures, Monsieur, you have lost four hundred million francs in the gold pool this year." The official retorts indignantly, "We've been out of that thing since June. We haven't lost a sou."

Some of Fabra's scoops, however, suggest at least a second-hand source of information as to what is going on in the secret councils of the world's money managers. But Parisian newsmen competing with him are by no means convinced that his source is in Paris; gossip points to a neighboring capital. A secret shared by a large number of governments is a fairly dubious risk at best. (Where did BBC get its tip?) Here we have important monetary developments being considered by, say, seventy-five high officials in eight countries. All of these men are expected to resist the temptations to blab to their cronies, to consult important banking interests, and to phone their brokers.

* I know only four American foreign correspondents sufficiently specialized in monetary affairs to have done this. At the time of the devaluation crisis, one was in New Delhi, one was at a seminar in Turin, one was covering New York City finances, and the fourth, by his own published account, was at a house party in New Jersey, covering the story by telephone, with a highball in his hand. On the scene, in Europe, the great upheaval had to be covered for our press by reporters who couldn't tell the difference between a Roosa bond and a pawn ticket.

We must add that most of these men were being forced to support a policy opposed to their own convictions. That goes for the Americans as well; William McChesney Martin is hardly an advocate of a deficit, whether in foreign payments or in the budget. But when Congress and the White House fail to restore a balance, all Martin can do is raise interest rates, though seldom as much as he'd like. His West European confrères, who long ago put *their* accounts into balance, are openly bitter about having to supply the candles that the United States and Britain were burning at both ends. A common complaint has been that it was the debtors, not the creditors, who were calling the tune. The Europeans vetoed some of the wilder proposals brought by Washington but went along, grumbling, on one desperate makeshift after another. A basic monetary reform, they told one another, would have to wait until after the November election. Each time, they had to pretend that they *believed* in what they were doing or were pretending to do. This is what made it seem that only France was out of step. It is amusing now to read some of the dispatches of reputable reporters covering our recent monetary mishappenings. I cannot resist offering this one, dated March 10, 1968:

The steel-nerved decision today of the central banks of the United States and six European countries in the ancient Rhine River city of Basel, Switzerland, may have marked the beginning of the end of gold as a monetary metal.

The seven central bank chiefs decided, in effect, to let speculators have gold rather than give up the international monetary system, based on fixed exchange rates among currencies, that has been a major element in the prosperity of the industrial world. The system has depended, in the last analysis, on the convertibility of the United States dollar into gold at $35 an ounce. And that convertibility will remain.

That steel-nerved decision lasted just four days—if indeed there was such a decision. The seven bankers had *announced* only that they would keep on doing what they had been doing, which was to sell gold to all comers at $35 an ounce. But nobody believed them except a few loyal reporters. People in the money markets asked the obvious question, "Was *that* all they went to Basel for?" And with what I am tempted to call nerves of steel, they bought all the gold they could lay hands on. By Thursday night, the London Gold Pool closed up shop, and a preposterous dual market was announced.

Actually, there was only one, the free market, but it suited the authorities to pretend they were still trading gold at $35 an ounce. This, I think, is not so much because they were ashamed to be openly breaking solemn international treaties as because it was almost impossible to break the news to the home folks in an election year. How could Washington explain its desperate measures to hold on to its dwindling supply of "barbaric metal," after having told newsmen so often that the stuff was worth $7 an ounce? And how were the newsmen to explain it to their readers? Well, that's simple enough. They can just blame de Gaulle.

# 4

# DE GAULLE AND LE DÉFI AMÉRICAIN

> *"In fifteen years, the third largest industrial power of the world may well be, not Europe but American industry in Europe. Already today, in the ninth year of the Common Market, the organization of this European market is essentially American."*
> —*opening lines of* Le Défi Américain, *by Jean-Jacques Servan-Schreiber.*

EVER SINCE Franklin D. Roosevelt replaced dollar diplomacy with the good-neighbor policy, Americans have regarded foreign investment as an unmixed blessing, and even as a duty on the part of the rich toward the poor. In fulfillment of this obligation, we have risked the collapse of the dollar. We could withstand with sorrow but a clear conscience the base ingratitude of a few Latin-American intellectuals, Arab firebrands, and Charles de Gaulle. We had the moral support of the only people whose opinion we care at all about—the members of the Western Alliance. Now suddenly all this has changed. Our best friends are talking of our investment as a poisoned gift.

The turn was symbolized by the phenomenon of the 1967–68 publishing season in Europe. This was the extraordinary impact of a book called *Le Défi Américain*, which means literally "The American Challenge" but registers clear overtones of an American menace. In France, its appearance pushed all other new books out of the limelight, including even André Malraux's first important literary work in twenty years. The publisher claimed a nonfiction record, with sales of 500,000 in the first six months. I reserve judgment on the accuracy of the figure, in view of the fact that my own noncommittal news report on Le Défi was mistranslated in advertisements to appear as a rave review. But there can be no question of its broad circulation among businessmen, executives, engiders, intellectuals, and public officials. I have seen a copy in the black Citroën of a cabinet minister, and de Gaulle himself is said to have discussed it with intimates. (Asked to comment on it at a news conference, he smilingly replied, "Ici, on ne fait pas de publicité littéraire.") "Défi Américain" became a catch phrase of political discussion in western Europe. It was likely to come up in any talk on economic growth, the technological gap, even university reform. It was taken up with enthusiasm by the anti-Gaullist Atlantic Party in Europe, including the chiefs of the opposition in France. Harold Wilson adopted its argument that Britain must be admitted into the Common Market if Europe was to resist being overwhelmed by American power.

The success of Le Défi Américain made an international celebrity of its author, Jean-Jacques Servan-Schreiber. The young scion of a wealthy and politically active family which is not offended when it is likened to the Kennedys, Jean-Jacques was already a prominent figure. He had started his career on the Left, and won wide attention for his opposition to the Algerian war. His magazine L'Express, transformed by him from a left-wing tabloid into a Gallic Time Magazine, was a great success, although less and less appealing to the Left. And even while he was compiling Le Défi Américain, he was preparing to launch *L'Expansion*, styled after *Business Week*, for sale only to executives, who were assured that, like *Business Week*, it would not be offered to hoi polloi on the newsstands. (The author of *Le Défi Américain* does not labor the point that McGraw-Hill owns 49 percent of the stock in his newest venture.)

Endowed with blond good looks, slender, fluent, grave, and charming, Servan-Schreiber recalls to audiences the personality of John F. Kennedy, who remains, incidentally, more popular in France than he ever was in America. Servan-Schreiber enhances the resemblance with a modified crew haircut. But there is a certain obliqueness in his intellectual processes which, if not foreign to the Kennedys, is closer to Bobby than to Jack. On a panel show, for example, he was asked about the Vietnam war; he replied that it was deplorable, that the United States was in error, and that Europe was morally correct in condemning it, but that such condemnation was futile because nobody would listen to a Europe that was divided and weak, and this in turn was a result of Europe's failure to unite and build computers and schools of business administration. This failure, by implication, was largely the fault of de Gaulle. (Servan-Schreiber in *L'Express* was the first, to my knowledge, to accuse de Gaulle of surrendering France to United States hegemony.) This obliqueness of argument is often, but not always, effective. When Servan-Schreiber began a speech at the University of Madrid by deploring the dearth of liberty in Spain and ended by calling upon Europe to establish closer economic ties with the Franco regime, students mobbed him.

The success of *Le Défi Américain* is all the more remarkable in that it is not particularly profound or original. The marks of the editor's scissors are clearly visible. Whole chapters are borrowed—candidly, I hasten to note—from such authorities as the economist Edward Denison, Defense Secretary Robert McNamara, Jacques Maisonrouge of IBM, and Herman Kahn, the man who made the unthinkable nuclear holocaust thinkable. The contribution of Servan-Schreiber was journalistic technique and perfect timing. He packaged and offered a product just when the market was ready for it—that is, just when Western Europe was awakening to the fact that it was becoming an economic colony.

The fact, as presented by Servan-Schreiber, is not disputed and will not be labored here. The American stake in Europe *is* enormous (his figure of $14 billion is probably an underestimate) and growing fast. In key sectors, American companies *are* already predominant (computers, 80 percent of the market) or becoming so (semiconductors, 50 percent). The debatable area of *Le Défi Américain* is its analysis of why Europe is becoming satellized and what if anything should be done about it.

Its thesis is, briefly, that American business is taking over Europe not merely because it is richer and more advanced but also because it is better managed and, paradoxically, more "European-minded" than native business; Europe can stand up to this challenge, or menace, only by adopting the American virtues of bigness and scientific management, and that can be achieved only by a European government able and willing to reeducate European business. Thus de Gaulle, by blocking the unity of Europe, renders it helpless to resist American encroachment.

This thesis is now broadly accepted by the Atlantic Party and by American businessmen and diplomats in Europe; those Americans there who have read *Le Défi Américain* are among its most enthusiastic boosters. There is certainly considerable truth in it, and it is evidently flattering to Americans. But flattery can be embarrassing. Servan-Schreiber's admiration for American business leads him to what would seem a fairly excessive respect for the new sciences of marketing and management, and for their fountainhead, the Harvard School of Business Administration. He goes so far as to suggest that a German steel man, for example, will build a new mill without troubling his bullet-shaped head over whether he will be able to sell the product, whereas an American firm would not dream of investing in a plant before it had scientifically forecast the market for twenty years ahead. Hence, Servan-Schreiber is certain that Europe's hope rests on the establishment of a Continental chain of Harvard-type SBA's. This is a view also favored at business forums. When David Rockefeller visited Paris for one of the Chase Manhattan Bank's annual sessions, he commented that, if Europe was falling behind, the cause could be discerned from the fact that there were no words in French for "marketing and management." Leaving philology aside, I asked one of his bright young aides whether Rockefeller's grandfather, John D., knew the words "marketing and management." I received only a small smile.

Although Servan-Schreiber is the highly educated and intelligent product of a society that regards itself as the virtual inventor of logic, he is subject here to the vulgar error of *post-hoc* reasoning: Americans chew gum, Americans are rich— Q. E. D., one becomes rich by chewing gum. As Thorkil Kristensen, the secretary general of the OECD, commented not long after *The Défi Américain* appeared, America began her extraordinary expansion in the nineteenth century, *before* the science explosion (and certainly before the Harvard Business School). American business, he said, made America rich enough to afford these luxuries and not vice versa. (I once asked two successful young alumni of the Harvard Business School what they had gained there. They looked at each other and laughed. One replied for both of them: "Contacts.")

Without rejecting out of hand the postwar business "sciences," one may observe that they are something less than infallible. If corporate decisions are now made by teams of certified managers armed with computers, slide rules, and market surveys, they are nonetheless capable of blunders on a more magnificent scale than ever before. So highly rated a manager as Robert McNamara, the "human computer," did not prevent Ford from blowing a quarter of a billion dollars on the Edsel.

The qualities of American business that have helped it to succeed in Europe were present long ago. American executives tend to be more adaptable, bolder and quicker to make a decision than the heads of European family-controlled businesses. The Americans also are, paradoxically, far more "Europe-minded." One foreign country is no better or worse than another to them; once established abroad, a company naturally wants to maximize its markets, doesn't it? Servan-Schreiber states the obvious when he says that in the Common Market, it is mainly American companies that have established international operations. Europeans are attached by caution, tradition, and sentiment to their countries, their towns and their homes. They resist the appeals of their governments to establish plants in backward areas—what Milanesi would want to live in Calabria, and who would exchange Paris for *le province*? The authorities have found American companies more willing to make the move. Also, cartels and other cozy arrangements are the rule in Europe, and family businesses that have flourished for generations by playing the game are reluctant to change. I am told that a great American company had to threaten its German executives with dismissal to force them to buy a Dutch steel that was cheaper than the Ruhr product. In spite of the dreams of the founders of the Common Market, there have been few mergers across the frontiers. The only important one so far has been the marriage of Agfa and Gevaert, the big photographic firms. The legal complexities of the fusion were such that they remain separate entities, called Agfa-Gevaert in Germany and Gevaert-Agfa in Benelux.

But the shortcomings of European businessmen and the virtues of Americans are, I think, only minor factors in the explosive growth of American business in Europe. The most obvious factors are of course the size, wealth, and technological power of our industry. An American company with an enormous market at home can take risks abroad that would be fatal to most European companies. (Servan-Schreiber mentions only American successes, never the inevitable failures.)

Further, foreign operations are often pure gravy. A company such as Corning Glass, which spent $30 million developing the television screen and long ago recovered its investment in the United States market, has an almost insurmountable advantage in Europe. It is far cheaper for European manufacturers to buy the screen from a Corning affiliate than to develop a rival process. Philips of the Netherlands has long tried to persuade other European firms to adopt European standards for electronic parts, which would reduce the Americans' advantage. This would require an expensive changeover, and so far the other firms have declined to go along.

Servan-Schreiber argues that the wealth of American companies is beside the point. He cites an American study showing that only 10 percent of the new money invested by Americans in Europe in 1965 came from the United States—and this sum was exceeded by dividends flowing home! The other 90 percent came from borrowings in Europe, subsidies by European governments, and the earnings of American subsidiaries in Europe. He adopts here the old Gaullist complaint that the United States is buying Europe's industry with Europe's own money. "Why them and not us?" he demands. Because, he replies, American management is better, and so forth.

If he had lingered on the question, he might have found that it was a little more complicated than that. True, European investors and, more tragically, those of the poorer countries of the world have long preferred American securities to their own. This is certainly due in part to the wealth and power of the American economy, and also to the role of the SEC in making Wall Street, against its will, an attractive place to invest money. (European market legislation is still primitive, and secrecy is sacred to European businessmen. An executive of a big French company once swore to me that he did not know how much money it earned. I believe him.) But a very large role in the siphoning of foreign money into American business is played by United States Government policy.

That the government picks up most of the tabs for developing American technology needs no emphasis here. Less well understood is the way our monetary system works for us. This point, overlooked by Servan-Schreiber, has been central to the Gaullist critique for years. It was expressed by the general himself, with his customary shocking bluntness, in his news conference of November 27, 1967:

It is true that we are confronted with an American grip on certain of our enterprises, but we know that that results in large part not so much from the organic superiority of the United States as from the inflation of the dollars they export to others under the cover of the *Gold Exchange Standard* [in English]. It is quite remarkable that the total of the annual deficits of the American balance of payments since eight years ago is precisely the total of American investments in the countries of Western Europe. There is here evidently an exterior, artificial, unilateral element, which weighs upon our national patrimony, and you know that France desires that this abuse be put to an end in the interest of the whole universe, and even in the interest of the United States, for which the payments deficit and inflation are deplorable, as they are for the whole world.

One may question one or another detail of this indictment, but no expert would challenge that there is some truth in it. Because of our own expansion and the weakening of Europe in two world wars, our dollar has become *the* world currency, used not merely for settling accounts but also as a reserve, equivalent to gold, for other currencies. For many years this enabled us, unlike other countries, to spend more money abroad than we earned from abroad; the excess dollars piled up in foreign treasuries or were lent back to us. This was a very good deal, but it could not last forever. Increasingly, foreign holders turned dollars in for gold, and by the early 1960's, a serious monetary crisis was under way, although only the experts were aware of it. The Kennedy Administration took the first serious step to reduce the dollar outflow in 1963, and it was a revealing one. This was the so-called Interest Equalization Tax, a penalty measure that, in effect, barred Americans from buying European stocks and bonds. (One result was a heavy decline of the European securities markets, which lasted for years. Europeans were of course encouraged to continue buying American securities.) There at the same time a significant exemption: An American company would not have to pay the tax if it bought 10 percent or more of the stock in a foreign company. Thus, while Washington was prohibiting American individuals from buying piddling amounts of European securities, it encouraged them to buy large controlling blocks! It was only when the monetary crash was upon us that President Johnson on January 1, 1968, forbade American companies to send their own money to Europe and ordered them, under penalty of law, to send more dividends home. (The latter decree appears to conflict with European law. As Finance Minister Michel Debré quickly pointed out, American subsidiaries in France are registered as French companies, with equal duties and equal rights to government subsidies and loans. A French stockholder in such a company could easily challenge a change in dividend policy decreed by a foreign government.) Even so, an important amendment was soon issued. This permitted American companies to *guarantee* repayment of bonds issued by subsidiaries in Europe. The companies had no trouble then in raising investment capital on the European market.

Our determination to continue tapping foreign resources of capital was paralleled by a similar determination to continue tapping foreign resources of human talent. The Immigration Act of 1965 ended the shameful quotas in favor of Nordic aliens; it substituted a priority to immigrants with skills useful to the American economy: scientists, engineers, doctors, nurses, and even cooks. It is a very costly affair for any country to rear and to educate such talent, only to have it put to work in a foreign land. A United Nations study found that even before the 1965 act, the United States was importing five thousand engineers a year, that it already was employing 20,000 foreign physicians, and that these numbers could only grow, since the American demand for engineers and physicians was far inferior to the output of our universities. Much, perhaps most, of this talent comes from poor countries. (The British "brain drain" has been the most highly publicized one, but it is seldom noted that Britain itself more than replenishes its talent supply by drawing on that of the Commonwealth.) The poor countries find themselves in a vicious circle: Their young talent is lured away by the better salaries and opportunities available in the United States, and they cannot offer better inducements at home, in part because of their dearth of skilled personnel. France is more resistant to foreign lures than most (though her cooks are in great demand), partly because she is a rich and attractive country, and most Frenchmen see no good reason to roam. But the pressure is there. Several years ago an American manufacturer of farm machinery took over the last independent French tractor firm, which had been facing bankruptcy. One of its first cost-cutting moves was to eliminate the research department, which only duplicated work being done at home. Some thirty technicians were dropped. No doubt they would have lost their jobs anyway if the Americans had not moved in, but the company's impending failure was certainly related to the competition of other American tractor firms already located in Europe. I was returning from a very impressive French rocket launching in Hamaguir, Algeria, when I asked a young member of the space research team what it would do if the government did not appropriate funds for further experiments. He shrugged and replied, "We'll go to work for Boeing, maybe?" Despite criticism of the whole *force de frappe* and space program by Servan-Schreiber and others, the funds *were* appropriated.

Until quite recently, Americans in Europe were fond of telling critics that foreign investment had never done *us* any harm—that, in fact, our industrial revolution was largely financed by Europe. They overlooked the difference that European investments hardly ever took the form of control of our industry. Up to World War I, Europeans bought American bonds chiefly; since then, well-heeled foreigners have loaded up on stocks, but hardly ever to the point of being able to dictate to American boards of directors. American foreign investment, by contrast, overwhelmingly demands control of the companies involved. As a result, many countries are witnessing a steady erosion of their sovereignty over their own economies, and see themselves slipping into the position of Canada, a majority of whose industry now belongs to Americans. It is argued that, thanks to this industry, the Canadian standard of living also approaches that of the United States. But this does not totally satisfy patriotic Canadians or patriotic Europeans. Pierre Uri, the research chief of the Atlantic Institute, has cited the way General Motors divides the world market among its subsidiaries: Holden of Australia may not sell to Japan, Vauxhall of England may not sell to the United States, Opel of Germany may not sell to Canada. "I think Europe has the right to say it does not accept this direction of exports, this division of markets by a foreign company," he declared. He went on to urge that subsidiaries be allowed to compete freely, "not only with other affiliates of the same company, but even with the parent company itself." One wonders what Walter Reuther would think of this.

It is a merit of *Le Défi Américain* that it should close the discussion on the tenet that foreign investment is an unmitigated blessing. One must acknowledge the extraordinary achievements of such investment (although when W. R. Grace & Co. acquired a hamburger chain in France, it was a bit difficult to discern the social or economic benefits to be gained). But now, in the midst of a world monetary crisis, it is clear that there is a price to be paid for unrestrained expansion. And I am afraid that in the future there may be increasingly a political price to be paid. In my presence one day, an unusually brash American investor blithely told the publisher of a French financial journal that in ten years the United States would own Europe. The publisher, an exceedingly mild man, blinked and responded softly, "Eh bien, monsieur, if that day comes, why, we shall have to take it back."

I am convinced that there is a point, varying from country to country, in which the growth of American investment may be positively dangerous to the interest of the United States. Clearly, however, this growth is not something that the United States can easily control. It is hardly desirable to order American businessmen not to invest where they please, although we have come close to that in our belated and inadequate effort to preserve the $35 price of gold. We might, perhaps, shift our emphasis from the active promotion of private investment to a more active extension of aid to poorer countries. But in the end, obviously, whether other nations preserve their economic independence will depend on their own efforts.

For Servan-Schreiber, the solution is clear: a federated Europe, with a political authority able to create Harvard Business Schools and agencies for the development of computers, atomic energy, and so on. Since he allows for national sovereignty within this federation, the whole is rather reminiscent of de Gaulle's *Europe des Patries*; the only evident difference being that Servan-Schreiber would immediately include Britain, Ireland, and Scandinavia (and perhaps Spain). It is also rather reminiscent of the Common Market itself. The Common Market already has an atomic-energy agency which, unfortunately, is paralyzed by the conflicting aims of member countries. It also has a central administration, called the Commission. De Gaulle did, as it happens, propose in 1962 to endow it with a sort of consultative government, comprising the six chiefs of state, which would harmonize their policies on foreign, economic, cultural, and military affairs. This *Plan Fouchet* was rejected by the Atlanticists, led by the Dutch, who saw in it a rival to NATO.

The Common Market also has buried, up to now, all proposals for a common policy on limiting foreign investments—that is, American investments. Servan-Schreiber alludes to the celebrated affair of the General Motors plant. GM wanted to build it at Strasbourg. Giscard-d'Estaing, who was Finance Minister at the time, stalled on granting a permit. Tired of waiting, GM chose a site in Belgium, instead. France lost the payroll and the tax revenues from the new plant, but as a Common Market member she could not keep the GM cars from competing freely in France with the native product. (Belgium's attitude is understandable; since she has no auto industry of her own, an assembly plant is a total gain. Her appetite for foreign investment is insatiable. When President Johnson cut off the flow of American investment funds in 1968, Belgium offered to lend American companies the full cost of new plants, at little or no interest.) The GM affair is cited to prove the futility of trying to block United States investment by legal barriers, but it could as well be cited to prove the futility of the Common Market. With six members, the market has enormous difficulty in reaching decisions on relatively minor issues and in making its decisions stick. (Were it not for de Gaulle's insistence that important questions be decided only by unanimous vote, the market would have broken up long ago.) What in the world makes Servan-Schreiber think it would be easier to reach such decisions with eleven members? And if the purpose is to emulate the United States, why is the Common Market, with a population equal to that of the United States, not big enough?

*Because there is no such thing as big enough.*

All Europe is convinced of the virtue and necessity of bigness. That goes for the de Gaulle regime, incidentally. When it abandoned its effort to keep American investment out, it mounted a campaign for mergers among French companies, to make them big enough to compete. The conclusion that bigness will turn the trick is of course drawn from the American experience. But as often happens, the lesson is incomplete. Our European admirers overlook, for example, the role our antitrust laws have played in promoting our industrial growth.

It is true that, *all things being equal*, the big guy will beat the little guy every time. Studebaker built as good a car as GM did, sometimes a better one, and could sell it as cheaply. But it could not compete with GM's advertising budget and dealer network. Size here did not produce a better product, it just smothered the opposition. Still, it was not lack of size alone that killed the Studebaker, but lack of common sense. I take no special credit for having warned in the *Atlantic Monthly* more than ten years ago that Studebaker would lose if it tried to beat the big three car companies on *their own ground*. Studebaker had been a pioneer in compact cars and in rakish, sporty design. It abandoned these fields to the imports and devoted its last resources to building the same fantailed bathtubs all other red-blooded American firms were producing.

Our business history offers many happier stories, of little guys who beat big guys because they were quicker and sharper. Control Data has made it in the computer field by finding an area neglected by IBM; General Electric has tried to challenge IBM all along the line and is floundering.

What is true for companies is true for nations. Sweden, with a population 4 percent that of the United States, has achieved a standard of living comparable to ours; the products of her specialized industries enjoy worldwide markets. Japan, with hardly any resources other than a population half as large as ours, and with no history in science, technology, or "marketing and management," has achieved the fastest economic growth rate in the world. Neither of these countries, incidentally, has yielded any important part of its industry to American control. Servan-Schreiber discusses both these success stories in an appendix, saluting the role of free enterprise and good labor relations. Yet he manages to overlook their most striking lesson: that it is not necessary to be as big as the United States to succeed.

The best proof of that is the United States itself. We had a population of less than four million in 1790, when Tom Paine told his fellow Englishmen that the American workman lived better than they did. Our industrial revolution was in full stride before 1880, when we reached a population of fifty million—that of France today.

Contrary to the popular assumption, there are few industries that demand a continental scale to survive. Britain, France, Italy, West Germany, and even Sweden all support profitable automobile industries. Considerable European steel is sold in the United States, over the violent complaints of a protectionist steel lobby. In many areas of chemicals and machine tools, European technology is at least competitive with ours. As for those enterprises that *may*—I repeat, *may*—be beyond the capacity of any single West European country, there is little reason to believe that a twelve-country agency is the best way to undertake them. The areas most often mentioned are computers, aviation, atomic energy, and space communications. No serious international effort has been mounted in computers (though France is making a costly and belated effort to re-create an independent industry). There *are* European space and nuclear programs, but they just sputter along, with most members satisfied to depend on American leadership. Only France has maintained a strong independent effort in these fields. In aviation, the most promising joint developments have been Franco-British, with the French providing most of the drive. They have sought to bring the Germans in on the proposed European airbus, but Lufthansa prefers to buy American, it seems.

"The most successful of the enterprises of cooperation is the construction of the forthcoming supersonic airplane Concorde," Servan-Schreiber says. But he makes the acknowledgment only to demonstrate that this kind of bilateral deal on specific projects will not do. He recalls the hesitations of the British; he could even, if he cared, have gone further and shown that the plane would have got off the ground quicker and cheaper if only *one* country had been involved, instead of two. But his objective is to prove that *any* effort to keep up with the United States is absurd, unless it is conducted by a European government that has retrained a new generation of managers and technicians. The Concorde may indeed, he admits, be the first commercial supersonic aircraft—but it is already obsolete by comparison with the Boeing 2707! The Boeing will be bigger and quicker and slicker, he declares.

It would be difficult to find a better example of what de Gaulle has called the "passion for national abasement." It is, after all, obvious that a plane coming off the line in 1972 will be more modern than one flown in 1968. French patriotism, or even Europe-mindedness, might have suggested another observation: that President Johnson decided to build an American supersonic airliner with government funds (the aviation industry having refused to put up any substantial contribution of its own) only *after* the Concorde project was definitely under way—in order not to lose American leadership in this field. If the French and British had not taken the initiative, there would have been no supersonic transport. But Servan-Schreiber does not make this observation, because his real target is not the American challenge, but the Gaullist challenge.

There are many conceivable roads toward economic growth in independence: the Swedish way, the Japanese way, and even the Russian, Chinese, and Cuban ways. They share one common denominator: a strong national will, which is lacking from Servan-Schreiber's prescription. It may well be that, from the long-range interest of the United States, the de Gaulle way is as good as any.

# 5

# DE GAULLE AND BRITAIN

*"It was the economic crisis of 1961, when every Tory measure had failed to bring economic security and independence for Britain, that drove Mr. Macmillan into his panic application to enter the Common Market, on terms which everyone now recognizes would have meant the total disruption of our trade with the Commonwealth, and would have brought in this country unacceptable rises in prices and an intolerable burden on our balance of payments."*
*—Harold Wilson, February 20, 1965.*

AN AMERICAN MAY draw some small comfort from the knowledge that our British cousins are even more irrational about France than we are. I don't mean that they're pouring good claret down the drains; that's not their style. But they are quite daft on the subject just the same. This is actually a painful observation for an American like myself who had the privilege of serving with them in the Battle of the Atlantic. Many people have met danger with courage, but I think none have shown quite the same matter-of-factness about it. (On a recent French television program commemorating that epic, a white-haired British skipper was clearly embarrassed to be reminded of Churchill's ringing phrase about fighting on the beaches. "Of course we would have fought," he said. "But

67

we always thought those speeches were for export, don't you know?") Now I am not one of those many American and British journalists who insist that all that is finished, that Britons won't fight or even work anymore (how can they, when they're supposed to be up gambling and frugging all night?). But there is no blinking the fact that things have changed. The nation that turns away British subjects because of the color of their skin is not quite the same nation that invented fair play. It is a symbol of the change that a great many Britons now firmly believe that, if the trade figures are shocking, if the pound sterling has collapsed, if the natives east of Suez are restless, and if the hoof and mouth disease has stricken Devon, it is all the doing of those ruddy blighters across the Channel.

To be fair, the British have rather better grounds than we have to be annoyed. It is never very pleasant to be blackballed, and being barred from the Common Market was acutely humiliating. Nobody likes foreigners, but the English have a noble contempt for them bred of centuries of world domination from their tight little isle ("FOG OVER CHANNEL—CONTINENT ISOLATED"). They never really wanted to join the Europeans; in fact, the Common Market was established in Rome in 1958 against their violent opposition. Prime Minister Harold Macmillan was openly bitter about the pressure brought by the United States to bring the Common Market into being. He recalled that for centuries Britain had fought to keep the Continent—that is, France and Germany—from uniting, whether under the Bourbons, the Hapsburgs, Bonaparte, the Hohenzollerns, or Hitler. And he warned that if we insisted on integrating the Continent, Britain would have no choice but to organize a defensive alliance on the periphery. He even reminded us that, when Napoleon held sway over the Continent, Britain made an alliance with Russia. Macmillan did not actually go so far, but he did organize a peripheral alliance of seven countries against the Common Market—the European Free Trade Area (EFTA). Then, when Macmillan finally decided in 1961 to join the club of the Six—provided, he said, that the rules were waived "to meet the special needs of the United Kingdom, of the Commonwealth, and of the EFTA"—why, de Gaulle wouldn't have him! The humiliation contributed to the election victory of Labour, which in the main had opposed the Common Market as a capitalistic league sponsored by the United States and as an instrument of the cold war. In 1962, the Labour leader Hugh Gaitskell was warning that British entry would mean "the end of Britain as an independent nation . . . the end of one thousand years of history and the end of the Commonwealth," while Harold Wilson was saying that "the whole concept of the Treaty of Rome is anti-planning, at any rate anti-national planning." The following year, Candidate Wilson saw "even more signs now in the Common Market . . . that it is becoming inward looking and restrictionist and protectionist." But by 1967, Prime Minister Wilson was knocking on Europe's door again. With the same result. It is interesting to note that his chief door knocker, Lord Chalfont, made essentially the same threat in 1967 that Macmillan made in 1960. In his famous briefing of British newsmen at Lausanne, Chalfont warned that, if Britain was excluded from the Common Market, it might have to reconsider its commitments, including its presence in Germany. The threat, which was effectively to break up the Western Alliance, brought the witty comment of a Gaullist deputy that an English gentleman applying for admission to a club did not say he would burn the house down if he was barred.

In fact, the most striking thing about Britain's two efforts to enter the Common Market is how *un-British* they were. This is especially true of the second trip, because Wilson can hardly have had any illusion about how it was going to turn out. As the wartime posters demanded, was this trip really necessary?

When I think of what the Common Market is all about, I think of the fishermen of Concarneau. They had been on strike for three weeks when I got there, and the medieval Breton port was choked with rusting trawlers. They were demanding a sixteen-hour day and a minimum wage, but the strike was really over the Common Market. Fishermen are paid in shares of their catch; for many months, prices at the dockside auctions, called *criées* or shouts, had been disastrously low. A major reason was the competition from the fast-growing fishing fleets of Belgium, the Netherlands, and above all West Germany. Their taxes were lower than those paid by the French trawler operators, their social security charges were less, and their boats, subsidized by their governments, were more up-to-date. Their ports of landing from the North Sea are often closer to Les Halles in Paris than are the Breton ports. And under the Treaty of Rome, there was little France could do to prevent the foreign fish from undercutting her own market, and nothing she could do immediately about the other countries' subsidies. "We have a free-trade area in fish," a Concarneau man complained, "but not a Common Market."

This elementary and crucial distinction seems to have been overlooked by many of those who pontificate about the Common Market. A free-trade area is a simple customs union, where goods pass across borders without hindrance. But free trade does not necessarily mean fair trade. A common market goes a big step beyond that by trying to harmonize taxes and subsidies and other national policies that may tilt the scale in favor of one competitor over another. This is far from simple to achieve. Our own country, often held up as a model to Europe, has never entirely accomplished it, as witness the problem of the runaway shop. Even among us, poor states are constantly luring industry from rich ones with tax exemptions, subsidies, and cheap labor. How can a united Europe prevent the standards of the more advanced countries from being lowered to those of, say, Italy? (The problem tends to solve itself eventually, as the poor regions become rich, but the process can be rough on those who lose their jobs.) The fear of such a "competition of the worst" was often cited by British labor as a reason to stay out of Europe, and it has been a lively concern of European labor as well. With cause, for as Wilson pointed out, the governments of Western Europe are all relatively conservative. Today, no demand for higher wages or more social welfare is put forward in Europe without meeting the objection that it would weaken the nation's ability to compete within the Common Market.

Now, the structure envisaged by the Treaty of Rome was not to be built in a day. In fact, it provided a ten-year period, 1958 to 1968, for the gradual elimination of barriers among the member countries (France, West Germany, Italy, Belgium, the Netherlands, and Luxembourg). Meanwhile, the Six undertook in scores of separate negotiations to iron out differences in their taxes, welfare, and subsidies, topic by topic and subject by subject, year by year. It is a fiendishly complicated chore, whose strains have several times threatened to tear the market apart, and it is not yet completed. There should be an agreement by the Six on fish, covering taxes, prices, and subsidies, but there isn't any. So the strike movement that began in Brittany has spread fitfully along the Norman and Aquitaine coasts, and the French fishing fleet continues to dwindle. The boatmen claim that their government sacrificed their fishing industry in exchange for agreements with the other five countries on grain, meat, and milk. I cannot say whether this is true (though I heard a bishop repeat the charge in a sermon in Fécamp), but that is precisely how trade agreements are reached—by a process of give and take. And it is inevitable that France, the largest agricultural producer in the Common Market, would put the interest of her farmers first, especially since, as she often pointed out, she was making the heaviest tariff cuts among the Six on industrial goods. (France, once the most protectionist of countries, has become under de Gaulle one of the most liberal. She has virtually eliminated curbs on capital movements, and has several times lowered tariffs unilaterally, to encourage competition and hold prices down.)

Ironically, however, the farmers are not visibly grateful. On the contrary, while the fishermen were striking, many thousands of farmers were demonstrating violently, from Brittany to the Midi. Violently is no exaggeration; hundreds of farmers and gendarmes were injured, many highways and railroads were blocked, and several *mairies* and *préfectures* were damaged. Again prices were what the noise was about, but again the Common Market was the fundamental issue. Talking to these farmers was a poignant experience. For years, they had been told by their leaders (mostly Radical Socialists, and nearly all good Atlantic partisans) that the Common Market was the Promised Land, in which prices would rise and their markets would expand sixfold (unless that reckless fellow de Gaulle upset the cart). Many farmers borrowed money to buy machinery, livestock, and land in anticipation. Now the preparatory decade was nearly over, the great day was dawning—and they learned suddenly that far from being better off, they were going to be worse off than before! In fact, many are doomed to lose their farms, which were not big enough—"not on a Common Market scale." This of course is the name of the game. Competition drives out the weak producers and encourages progress. But it is not pleasant to the poor farmer.

The orators had told them that the united Europe would open five more countries to them as markets. They neglected to add that it would open *their* country to five new competitors. (The British may not have considered this point as carefully as they might.) Further, the Rome Treaty was vague when it came to agriculture, so there was nothing in it to prevent West Germany, for example, from continuing to import cheaper foods from outside the Common Market, while subsidizing its own relatively small number of farmers (that is the British system of course), and all the while moving industrial goods into France under preferential conditions— there was nothing to prevent it except the iron will of de Gaulle. Time after time he threatened to pull out of the Common Market to defend his farmers' interests; twice his delegates went so far as to walk out.

The impression Western readers get from the headlines is that everybody was in step but de Gaulle. Before they condemn him, they should consider our "chicken war" against a rise in the Common Market poultry tariff. ("I did not come here to threaten," said Secretary of Agriculture Orville Freeman, "but we are not going to see our proper and historic export markets taken away.") Or they might consider the lobbying of the United States and Britain against the Mansholt Plan for a Common Market policy on grain prices. (Freeman's tactics, *The New York Times* reported, brought mounting "criticism of the United States for unwarranted and untimely interference in European affairs.") These battles are too complicated to unravel here; the point is that each country defends its own interest.

Among the Six, France is the only country producing enough grain and meat to feed herself and export a substantial surplus. The other five, like Britain, have to import grain and meat, and they naturally prefer the cheapest source, whether it's the United States, Canada, or New Zealand. When it comes to citrus fruit, only Italy is an exporter in the Common Market, so it was up to Italy to keep Spain and Turkey from striking too advantageous a deal with the Six. Which Italy did. She blocked these countries from association (a modified customs-union arrangement) with the Common Market until her interests were protected. And nobody abused her for it.

De Gaulle did not win all his battles in the Common Market. He did win on grains, and the French grain producers were not among those who were stoning the prefectures. He did not do so well on poultry, which is why the feathers literally flew as angry chicken raisers used dead birds as projectiles. He has got nowhere so far on fish and has made only uneven progress on meat, milk, and vegetables.

But all that France *had* been able to accomplish would have been thrown back into contention had the Common Market begun seriously to consider the admission of Britain. As Couve de Murville pointed out, even to *negotiate* with Britain would have paralyzed all the complex and painful negotiations going on within the Common Market. It should be kept in mind that, if Britain went in, so would Ireland, Denmark, Sweden, Norway, and possibly several other countries. The problems of meat and chicken subsidies and all the rest would have to be gone over again—this time with eleven or more countries instead of six.

It is a commentary on journalism that the following statement may come as a surprise: *Britain never offered to join the Common Market as is.* Wilson was a little more coy about it in 1966–67 than was Macmillan in 1962–63, but both demanded negotiations to waive the rules in Britain's favor. They had to. Britain was in no shape at either time to switch from cheap to dear food supplies or even to drop all her barriers against Continental goods. She was in fact bankrupt and, if admitted to the economic union, would need special help from the Six, all of whom had sound currencies and healthy reserves. In May, 1961, Macmillan said candidly that it would be "quite impossible" for Britain to sign the Treaty of Rome. By July, he was ready to join "if satisfactory arrangements can be made to meet the special needs of the United Kingdom, of the Commonwealth, and of the EFTA." De Gaulle warned repeatedly and plainly that France would not sacrifice her agriculture and that Britain was not ready. But Macmillan pushed ahead until he got his veto in January, 1963. Belgium, Holland, and Italy then berated France and threatened a boycott of Common Market negotiations, but soon simmered down. (Germany's position is often difficult to assess. Speaking of the British application, Adenauer had said: "I am for it, but it is my task to represent not British interests but those of Germany. I must examine how far these interests are reconciled.") Anyhow, as long as de Gaulle was there, the other Common Market members could be as friendly as they liked to the British cause. There was no prospect of actual admission, which would have forced them to reexamine their positions in detail.

The parallel of 1966–67 with 1962–63 is hallucinating.

Actually, Britain was in much worse shape than four years earlier, and hence an even more dubious candidate for membership, whether from her own point of view or from that of the Common Market, which was now considerably advanced in its internal arrangements. On May 31, 1965, Prime Minister Wilson told the House that, on grain alone, joining the Common Market would cost Britain something like $280 million a year, which would "greatly increase our cost of living, therefore our wages and therefore our export costs, and the gain of getting under the tariff barrier would be lost." Not to mention that Continental products, such as German drugs and chemicals, would be getting into Britain under *her* barriers! On March 10, 1966, Wilson repeated: "We have stated our conditions. If we can get these terms, we will go in. If we can't, of course we shall not." A week later, in Bristol, he told Labourites: "We must be free to go on buying food and raw materials, as we have for one hundred years, in the cheapest markets—in Canada, Australia, New Zealand, and other Commonwealth countries. . . . We reject any idea of supranational control over Britain's foreign and defense policies. We are in Europe, but our power and influence are not, and must never be, confined to Europe." Five weeks later, his government formally announced its readiness to join the Common Market, "provided that British and Commonwealth interests are safeguarded." But Foreign Secretary Michael Stewart added the sensible observation that first one should find out whether the lady was willing. Premier Pompidou came to London and said she was—if Britain "accepts the Treaty of Rome and the arrangements subsequently agreed." All observers agreed that this was imposible and in fact amounted to a turndown. De Gaulle soon dotted the i by publicly reviewing the reasons for his 1963 veto.

Wilson then began banging on the door of Europe. In Strasbourg, he declared that, if Britain did not get into the Common Market, "it will not be our fault." Chalfont warned of dire alternatives. Distinguished journalists took their passion and their bad manners as proof of their sincerity, but neither man ever spelled out his conditions for joining the Common Market. In fact, they must have known—all Europe had known for months—that they did not stand a chance. What they did accomplish was to strain relations among the members of the Common Market, to worsen British relations with France, and to give British voters the delusion that their economic problems would be solved if That Fellow would only let them through those pearly gates. A cynic would say it was an interesting distraction from Labour's failure on the home front.

Wilson's conduct recalls the judgment he himself had recently passed upon his predecessors. In that Bristol speech of 1966 he declared:

In 1963, when the present Conservative leader [Edward Heath] was negotiating for entry, Britain suffered an intolerable humiliation by the curt French refusal to allow Britain to join, even on the unacceptable terms the Conservative Government was ready, even willing, to see imposed upon it.

But the French refusal at that time was due to the inept handling of Anglo-French relations and the duplicity shown by the Tory leaders concerned. In the meetings with President de Gaulle at Rambouillet, they failed to deal straight with him. They failed to tell him that following the breakdown of the disastrous Tory Skybolt policy, they were about to go to the United States for Polaris submarines. It was the Nassau agreement that slammed the door of the Common Market in Britain's face.

Since the Labour Government came into office, we have worked to improve relations with the French Government. . . .

The reference was to the Kennedy-Macmillan meeting in Nassau in December, 1962, at which Britain abandoned its independent missile program and accepted American Polaris missiles instead, with American control over their use. (Duplicity is perhaps too strong a word, but there is a lingering odor about more than one aspect of the affair. The French insist that Macmillan had just sold the Continentals on a European space program that would use the British rockets as boosters. The French became its most enthusiastic promoters. Five years later, after many millions of dollars had been spent, London virtually abandoned the program, shattering French hopes for an all-European satellite communications system. Again, in French eyes, the British chose the cheaper American product.)

Wilson was probably laying it on a bit when he implied that it was the Nassau meeting that killed Britain's chances. But it did not improve them any. General de Gaulle himself publicly recalled the affair in 1966, when he was trying to discourage Wilson from making another vain application. The general reminded the world that he had vetoed British entry once. He went on: "Not that we despaired of ever seeing that great island people truly wed its destiny to that of the Continent, but the fact is that it was not then in a position to apply the common rules, and that it had just, in Nassau, sworn an allegiance outside of a Europe that would be a real Europe."

Here we leave economics behind and enter the political arena. And here the United States becomes a principal figure. As a matter of fact, it always was. The United States was an active sponsor of the Common Market, as it was of NATO, with the aim of strengthening West Europe against the Soviet bloc. There were idealistic motives, surely, but the cold war was a dominant consideration; early in the game, the State Department insisted on keeping out of the Common Market such neutrals as Austria and Sweden, while it tried to persuade a reluctant Britain to join. (State at the same time had the contradictory task of keeping the Common Market from hurting U.S. trade interests. One solution was the Kennedy Round of negotiations to lower tariffs.) We also pushed for political as well as economic fusion; de Gaulle retorted that "the nations that are becoming associated must not cease to be themselves." This was, oddly enough, welcomed in London as removing one of Britain's main reasons for opposing the Common Market, the threat of "supranational control."

When Macmillan finally let himself be persuaded to apply for membership, the White House announced its gratification, and it campaigned actively for Britain. It is a measure of the change in opinion in Europe that when Wilson applied four years later, the word went out to American diplomats in Europe to button their lips. We wanted Britain in, but a plug from us would no longer be helpful. An even more dramatic sign of the change was displayed by Wilson. In a 1963 broadcast he had said that the Common Market was "becoming inward-looking and restrictionist and protectionist, and what we would like to see, as President Kennedy has said, is a getting together on the Atlantic-wide basis, not just a narrow Europe." But on November 30, 1966, Wilson declared that he wanted Europe to be a "pillar of equal strength with the United States." He continued:

"Our American friends, because they are our friends, will understand when I say that, however much we welcome new American investment here as in other parts of Europe, there is no one on either side of the Channel who wants to see capital investment in Europe involve domination or, in the last resort, subjugation."

The first Wilson statement, made in 1963, states the original goal of the Atlantic Party (which on the Continent, just to confuse things, also calls itself the European Party). This goal was to merge all the West into one economic and political union. The second statement is the new line of the Atlantic Party, which is to merge all the West *except the United States* into one economic and political union, so as *to stave off domination by the United States*. This doctrine got its Bible later in *Le Défi Américain*, which pointed out that United States business was already in a commanding position within the Common Market. (Its solution was a huge non sequitur: Admit Britain to the Common Market and go on from there.)

Despite its apparent conversion, the British Government's attitude toward Europe vis-à-vis the United States remains ambiguous, to put it mildly. I would not go so far as The Washington *Post* which, in April, 1968, reported from London: "Britain has all but legally become the 51st State of the American Union." But surely, Britain under Labour has become more rather than less dependent on Washington. Macmillan felt able, for example, to resist and bury the Multi-Lateral Force pushed so hard by the State Department; we may speculate that, if he were still in power, he might have been less uncritical of our Vietnam policy than Wilson was. Whatever Wilson might say about independence, when the United States and the Common Market countries took opposing sides in the Kennedy Round and monetary talks (as occasionally happened), Wilson was on our side. This is fine for us (assuming that our official policies are good ones), and it may be unavoidable for Britain as long as her financial situation remains desperate. But it hardly supports the thesis that the admission of Britain would make Europe more independent of the United States.

Now it is good American doctrine that an independent Europe would be a good thing for the United States: It would permit us both to lighten our military burdens and devote greater efforts to easing poverty in the world. It is argued that once inside the Common Market, Britain would be able to take a more European position. But until she works out her economic and monetary problems, she cannot stand the shock of full membership and full competition in Europe. In light of this, it is hard to understand why she has steadfastly refused the repeated suggestions of France that she seek *association* with the Common Market—a transitional phase in which trade barriers could be gradually reduced.

As Labour said of the Tory government and as the Tories said of the Labour government, Britain's conduct in the dispute with France over the Common Market has been neither rational nor beneficial to Britain. De Gaulle's conduct *has* been rational and *has* been in the interest of France. It is also arguably in the long-range interest of Britain and the United States—though I would not suggest that that was de Gaulle's essential consideration. I should think that his profoundest motive was not economic but, as always, the independence and grandeur of France. From the Anglo-Saxon point of view, however, this is not necessarily bad.

# 6

# DE GAULLE THROWS US OUT

*"Since this division of the world between two great powers, and therefore into two camps, clearly does not benefit the liberty, equality, and fraternity of peoples, a different order, a different equilibrium are necessary for peace."*

—*de Gaulle, in a speech on April 27, 1965.*

AS WALTER LIPPMANN has observed, there are some notions that just close off any intelligent discussion. Such a one is the theme of French ingratitude: Twice we sacrificed our youth to save that country, and if she now disowns us— why, there's nothing more to be said.

But the truth is a bit more complicated, as always. The Yank who said, "Lafayette, we are here!" was oversimplifying things too. He was suggesting that the doughboys were simply repaying an old debt. It is correct that, although our textbooks do not labor the point, a French fleet, a French expeditionary force, and French arms and money did turn the tide for the American rebellion. But alas, they were not sent because Louis XVI was devoted to the cause of liberty; we simply happened to share a common enemy. Our gratitude did not prevent our young republic from going to the brink of war with our French allies a few years after independence. In this century, we have twice been allies again. But Americans tend to forget that in 1916, when a whole generation of Frenchmen and Britons was perishing on the Western Front, Woodrow Wilson was campaigning on the slogan "He Kept Us Out of War," and in 1940, when France was under the heel of the occupant and Britain was fighting alone for her survival, Franklin D. Roosevelt was promising the American electorate "again and again and again" that he would not send its sons to fight in a foreign war. It is not to minimize his generous spirit or his correct judgment of the issues to observe that, if Japan had not attacked us at Pearl Harbor and if Hitler had not immediately declared war, the course of our involvement against the Axis would have been different.

We are justifiably proud of the enormous contribution made by the American economy toward getting Europe back on its feet after the war. But it is not intellectually honest to deny the role played by the Red menace in getting the appropriations through Congress. (France, incidentally, spends a larger proportion of her wealth in foreign aid than we do; nobody would suggest that this is totally free of national self-interest.)

There *is* a tie between France and the United States; it is the tie not of savior and saved, but of allies who fought together in a common cause. Let us not measure who made the greater sacrifice, else we must consider our debt to the Russians. Few people would argue that we were ingrates and blaspheming their dead when we challenged Stalin's policies. An obligation that we do have, perhaps, is to listen with an open mind to the admonitions of our former comrades in arms. This we have not always done.

A variation on the theme of an ungrateful France is that of a vengeful de Gaulle. This one, too, is based on a superficial attention to history. It is true that we have been pretty tough on de Gaulle. When he refused to accept the defeat of France in 1940 and chose to continue the struggle in lonely exile, the State Department was not among those who rallied to his cause. State pinned its hopes on an ultimate conversion of the Vichy regime, and in its typical fashion clung to this policy long after it had been discredited. When de Gaulle won his first little victory by occupying the islands of St. Pierre and Miquelon just before Christmas, 1941, Secretary of State Cordell Hull publicly disowned this outrage of "the so-called Free French." (Privately, according to de Gaulle, Anthony Eden conveyed to him a threat by Washington to send a cruiser to take the islands back; the general replied that he would fight, and the matter was dropped.) It is true that we kept de Gaulle in the dark on the landing in North Africa, and tried for months afterward to maintain a quasi-Vichy regime there. It is true also that as late as the Yalta conference of 1945, we excluded de Gaulle, and hence France, from planning the shape of postwar Europe. Hence many journalists, who cannot find any rational explanation for France's policy since then, put it all down to spite for those wartime affronts.

It doesn't wash. De Gaulle may be a man who nurses a grudge, but that is hardly the dominant theme of his policy. That theme is no mystery: It is *la gloire de la France*. As a Frenchman, as *the* Frenchman par excellence, he has surely never forgotten that his country was thrice in three generations occupied and humiliated by Germany, yet when he thought it would serve the interest of France, he has embraced the Germans and saluted their noble traditions. He has been tougher toward the Russians than we were, and friendlier; he has backed the United States in some international crises, opposed it in others; he extended his arms in blessing to the

Algerian settlers and the rebel generals, and then broke them. De Gaulle (like FDR) may be accused of cynicism but not of sacrificing his country to avenge the memory of an old insult.

The spite theory has often been used to explain away France's opposition to the United States role in Vietnam. At least until that war reached its present level of unpopularity, it was fashionable to say that the French, having been defeated in Indochina themselves, did not want to see *us* win there. This seems plausible, but it collapses before one embarrassing fact: The only Frenchmen who have defended our Vietnam war effort also defended the French war in Indochina. The few hundreds who demonstrated in sympathy with us were rallied by the extreme right—the French equivalents of the John Birchers and the Rockwell fringe. Those Frenchmen who opposed the Nazi occupation, the attempt to reconquer Indochina, and the Algerian repression have been unanimously opposed to the American policy in Vietnam. This lineup was more or less the same throughout West Europe. If de Gaulle was the first chief of state in West Europe to reprimand our Vietnam policy, with a severity that grew as we dug ourselves in deeper and deeper, it was only another example of his taking a shocking position that years later seems only to have been clairvoyant. Our other European allies generally refrained from offending our sensibilities; with few exceptions they politely endorsed our adventure, though none went so far as to send *their* own youths to die in Vietnam. Most loyal of all was Harold Wilson, who flouted his own Labour Party in upholding—only verbally, to be sure—every step of escalation decided by Washington. His service to the hawk faction in America was incalculable. His defenders argued that he was thus able privately to urge restraint upon Washington, whereas de Gaulle was sacrificing any possibility of acting as a mediator. In the event, Washington did not listen to either of them. In retrospect, one may ask which was our better friend, the one who flattered our folly or the one who denounced it.

Once we dismiss the notions of French ingratitude and spite, we may hope to examine reasonably the issue that brought about the split between the United States and France: NATO. I believe that the American complaint, accepted by nearly all organs of opinion on our side of the Atlantic, may be fairly summarized as follows: (1) NATO saved Europe from Soviet aggression; (2) de Gaulle abruptly pulled out, without giving us time to negotiate changes; (3) safe behind NATO's shield he builds an absurd atomic *force de frappe* that is balm to his ego but would deter nobody, that is too costly for France, and that encourages the Germans to seek an atomic capability of their own.

Well, let's see.

## NATO *saved Europe from Soviet aggression*

It is fairly easy to shoot large holes in this one. The North Atlantic Treaty—to which France, at this writing, still adheres —was signed only on April 4, 1949. It was and remains a pact of mutual assistance, declaring that "an attack against one . . . shall be considered an attack against them all" and pledging each signer in such an event to take only "such action as it deems necessary." It proclaims the determination of its signers "to safeguard the freedom, common heritage, and civilization of their peoples, founded on the principles of democracy, individual liberty, and the rule of law," and it pledges to promote "peaceful and friendly international relations by strengthening their free institutions." Considering that Portugal and Greece are signers, this now has an ironic ring. The treaty was, in fact, of course, drafted not to strengthen free institutions but to meet one specific threat—that of a Soviet attack on the West. When it was signed, the Greek civil war was virtually over and the Berlin blockade was more than a year old. These have been probably the most serious confrontations within Europe since the war—and we survived them without benefit of the North Atlantic Treaty.

NATO as we now think of it—that is, the integrated command of Allied forces which France has now abandoned—was not established until 1955. It would be difficult to prove that that integration had any more tangible result than the signing of the Warsaw Pact a week later. Before integration, the Allies stood helplessly by during the Berlin uprising of 1953; after integration, they stood helplessly by during the Hungarian uprising of 1956 and again during the building of the Berlin Wall in 1961. If Western Europe has been saved from a Soviet invasion, it was surely not because Luxembourg accepted a German general as commander of its troops, nor even because the German army was reestablished, but because of the American presence in Europe, backed by a nuclear deterrent. Neither of these has anything to do with NATO, really. NATO was a political device for rearming Germany without unduly upsetting our other allies. We are in Europe—that is, in West Germany—because of World War II, and we have always rightly refused to share with anyone the right to decide when our nuclear deterrent may be employed.

Cartesian logic, so beloved by the French, would demand that we begin at the beginning, and ask whether there was indeed a menace of Soviet aggression against the West. A revisionist school of historians has lately taken the negative. They argue that the cold war began not in 1946 but in 1917, with the Churchillian effort to "strangle the Bolshevik baby in its cradle." They hold, in effect, that it was the West that was more often than not the offending party, mounting a diplomatic and economic blockade of the Soviet Union and encouraging the Axis to turn its aggressive tendencies in that direction. The result, they say, was the Hitler-Stalin pact and the beginning of World War II—which was itself only a partial interruption of the cold war. It is not necessary to accept this thesis to acknowledge that the whole subject of responsibility for the East-West split needs reexamining. It is curious today, for example, to recall that Roosevelt's recognition of the Soviet Union in 1933 was an act of high political courage. It is generally accepted now that Soviet policy has been fundamentally nationalistic and hence, in the broad sense, defensive, at least since the mid-Twenties when Stalin overcame Trotsky and his policy of permanent revolution. This did not rule out aid to Communist parties abroad (though it often included restraints upon them). It did not rule out the imposition of Communist dictatorships upon East Europe after World War II. But it does suggest that the fundamental motive of Soviet policy has been not expansion but fear. Fear, above all, of a resurgent Reich. If this is true, then NATO, far from halting Soviet aggression, has been a constant incitement to the fears that inspired Soviet aggressiveness.

The central issue of the cold war has been the status of Germany. The wartime alliance of the Big Four came to a formal rupture in 1947 over Soviet demands for heavy reparations and for maintenance of a Communist regime in East Germany; this of course would have meant perpetuation of an economically weak and divided Reich. The West, having buried the Morgenthau plan which aimed in the same direction, opted for a strong and (at least for the record) a unified

Germany, under the Western economic and political system. Pending a Soviet surrender we to this day refuse, with only de Gaulle dissenting, to recognize Germany's postwar frontier with Poland.

There is no evidence, however, that de Gaulle's quarrel with NATO was inspired by a concern for Soviet sensibilities. He was, on the contrary, a hard-liner for as long as he thought Soviet power to be a major menace. During the second Berlin crisis of 1961–62, for example, he vigorously opposed the inclination of the Allies to "negotiate under threats." He also backed President Kennedy in the Cuban missile showdown of October, 1962. He observed afterward, it is true, that Europe had then risked becoming involved in a war arising from a quarrel in which they were not consulted. But it was only much later, when the tendency toward disintegration of the world Communist bloc was far advanced, that de Gaulle stopped talking in his blunt fashion about "the Soviet menace." Even so, he has continued openly to encourage the Poles, Rumanians, and Hungarians to follow his example in seeking national independence. It was the issue of independence, not the fading of the Soviet menace, that determined de Gaulle's break with NATO.

## The "abrupt" departure

As the last Americans were leaving Toul Air Force Base in Lorraine, a native complained to me that the French Government had made no plans to provide new jobs for workers being laid off. "After all," he pointed out, "they knew the Americans would not stay forever!" I am embarrassed now to say that the remark struck me speechless. Suddenly, it *did* seem unnatural that our troops should still be there, twenty-two years after the victory, protecting a continent that once again was rich and strong. And it seemed strange that we had no plans, and apparently no desire, ever to leave. The man was right, anyhow, in saying that everybody had had ample warning. As early as 1949, six months after the signing of the North Atlantic Treaty, de Gaulle was on record as declaring that "France must count upon herself" for her defense and recovery. To be sure, he was out of power then, but there is a degree of continuity in French policy, independent of political changes, which is often overlooked. With de Gaulle on the sidelines, it was the Fourth Republic that led the resistance within the Western Alliance to the rearmament of Germany. More precisely, a faction of the Fourth Republic. When Secretary of State Dean Acheson proposed in 1950 to revive the Wehrmacht (under a new name), the issue split Western Europe in two. One side was the Atlantic Party, which looked toward the United States for its defense and resources. The other may, at the risk of confusion, be called the European Party; it included not only the Communists, neutralists, and Gaullists but all those others to whom the memory of German aggression was as vivid as their fear of Soviet aggression.

To make the idea more palatable, Acheson devised a scheme for an integrated force called the European Defense Community. The argument was that, as long as the Germans were snugly swaddled in community discipline, they would behave. The EDC treaty was signed by all the members of NATO in 1952. There was considerable opposition in Britain and elsewhere, but ratification posed no critical problem until the arrival to power of Pierre Mendès-France, the *other* big man in France's postwar history. (During his brief regime in 1954 he ended the Indochinese war and put Tunisia on the road to independence. Had he stayed on, he might have saved the Fourth Republic. But the Republic, it seems, was beyond saving. A prefect confided to me not long ago, "Only twice have I been proud to be a functionary of France: under Mendès and under de Gaulle.") Mendès never openly opposed EDC, but against enormous pressure he refused to make ratification an issue of confidence in the government. Left to their own consciences and the need to defend themselves before the electorate, a majority of the Assembly voted *non*. Mendès was subjected to heavy abuse on both sides of the Atlantic. Apparently in order to calm the storm while he devoted his main energies to negotiating peace in Indochina, he proposed another form of military integration within the existing structure of the alliance. Thus, rather oddly, the man who defeated German rearmament in 1954 became its father in 1955. Posthumously, so to speak, for Mendès had by then been scuttled by his fellow ministers, all good Atlanticists. Washington's motive in this affair was to force the rich Germans to share the burden of their own defense. But there is a strong case to be made that rearming the Germans only heightened the menace it was supposed to avert. Certainly, it frightened the Russians and their allies. When ratification of EDC seemed imminent, they went so far as to offer to join NATO! We turned them down. When Bonn was admitted to NATO in May, 1955, the Communist bloc signed its own mutual defense treaty, the Warsaw Pact.

EDC was to have a remarkable parallel in the affair of the Multi-Lateral Force (or multilateral farce, as Gen. Pierre Gallois quickly dubbed it). This scheme was enunciated by President Kennedy in 1961, when he was apparently still distracted by the Bay of Pigs fiasco. It called for the organization of a "mixed-manned fleet," with crews of scrambled nationalities; later, a similar land force was dreamed up. From a military point of view, this Tower of Babel concept was of course an absurdity. But its aim was not really the defense of the West, at least not directly; it was to give West Germany a share of the nuclear deterrent. (In the words of Tom Lehrer's "Military Lullaby," "one of the fingers on the button will be German.") Washington's idea was that otherwise the Germans would insist on building their own atomic bombs. There have always been critics among us who have suggested that our continual effort to forestall German demands by meeting them halfway may only have incited such demands. In any case, MLF certainly frightened the Eastern bloc, at a time when its tendency to pull apart was growing. It also frightened the West. ("MLF will scare Brezhnev," Lehrer sang. "I hope he is half as scared as I.") But there was a decisive difference between the story of the EDC and that of the MLF in 1964: This time, we had the Fifth Republic, not the Fourth, to contend with. De Gaulle said firmly that France would have to be counted out. Washington characteristically refused to abandon a crumbling position at the cost of losing face. MLF was "indispensable," Ambassador Finletter told the NATO Council. "As goes this fleet, so may go the defense of the West." The United States, actively supported only by Bonn, pushed the idea of a Multi-Lateral Force without France. While de Gaulle hinted he would quit NATO in that case, the other NATO members, including Britain, dragged their feet. Chancellor Erhard suggested that Bonn and Washington go it alone, but this was a little too much. With some adroit maneuvering by the British, who proposed a careful study of alternatives, the "indispensable" MLF was quietly buried. The defense of the West does not seem to have suffered fatally; according to the Institute for Strategic Studies, the ground forces of the Atlantic Alliance in Europe in 1966 exceeded those of the Warsaw Pact, 3.2

million to 2.9 million, and we had overwhelming superiority to the Soviet Union in atomic missiles—the "overkill capacity." It is hardly to be wondered that some Americans, including former Supreme Allied Commander Eisenhower, were demanding that the United States forces in Europe be reduced.

De Gaulle had always been against an integrated command. It gave foreigners control over his country's destiny, and that hardly fit his *"certaine idée de la France."* Ending this situation was one of his first considerations in 1958, when the ministers of the Fourth Republic, terrified by their rebel generals in Algeria, called him out of retirement. Hardly had he returned to power when he wrote to President Eisenhower and Prime Minister Macmillan, proposing that they form a Western directorate of three to set global policy and decide whether to use the bomb. His audacity must have stunned Ike and Mac. It recalls Marshal Foch's legendary telegram: "My center is giving way, my right is retreating, situation excellent, I attack." (I have always regarded this tale, which I hope is apocryphal, as exemplifying the worst in the military tradition.) Here was de Gaulle, with a war on his hands in Algeria, his armed forces menacing revolt, his homeland on the brink of civil war, his economy on the verge of crisis— and he was demanding an equal voice as one of the Western Big Three! A decade later, this proposal would seem a bit less presumptuous. France is the happiest of the Western Big Three: She is at peace at home and abroad, her military caste has long since been brought to heel, her empire has been liberated in an orderly fashion, her production per capita is the largest in Europe, her money is sound, and her moral prestige in Asia, Africa, and Latin America is higher than that of any other country. We may well envy her situation now.

We may be forgiven for not having foreseen the dramatic changes that the last decade was to bring. But we can hardly describe de Gaulle's departure from NATO as abrupt. It began, actually, with Eisenhower's rejection of his demand in 1958 for an equal voice with the United States and Britain in deciding the questions of war and peace. Within months, de Gaulle announced that France would not permit atomic missiles on her soil except under her own control. Step by step, beginning with the Mediterranean fleet, he freed his forces from automatic control by the alliance. Meanwhile, as crisis succeeded crisis between East and West, he kept up a drumfire of demands for reform of NATO. It was "the right and duty of the European continental powers to have their own defense," he declared in 1961, because it was "intolerable for a great state to leave its destiny up to the decision and action of another state." The Europeans, in the direct line of a potential attack, have the right to know "with which weapons and under what conditions their overseas allies would join them in battle."

Nobody with any acquaintance with NATO would deny that the United States has always firmly held the reins. A dramatic example of this, often cited in France but hardly mentioned elsewhere, was our unilateral reversal of NATO's basic strategy. At the outset, this strategy, unanimously adopted by the NATO Council, was Dulles' famous doctrine of "massive retaliation," calling for the immediate use of the hydrogen bomb against the Soviet Union if the Red Army crossed the line. When the Soviet Union developed its own deterrent, this doctrine lost some of its charm. In February, 1961, Dean Rusk called publicly for "strengthening the non-nuclear aspects" of the Allied defense, and was reported to have sent a secret memorandum to McNamara proposing the use of conventional weapons to meet a Soviet attack, at least for a "breathing period." This became the McNamara doctrine of a "graduated response," and it quickly became the new strategy of NATO. There was no vote in the council, because so momentous a decision would have to be unanimous, and de Gaulle made plain that he would veto it, on the ground that it would doom Europe to become a bloody battlefield for the third time in this century. We may differ with de Gaulle on the strategy of deterrence, but we cannot dispute that this momentous decision for NATO was made in the U.S.A. It was only in 1967, after France's departure, that the remaining NATO defense ministers dutifully ratified what had been decided for them six years before.

On September 9, 1965, de Gaulle issued his first formal notice of his impending departure from NATO. "So long as the solidarity of the Western peoples appears to us necessary for the eventual defense of Europe, our country will remain the ally of her allies," he said, "but upon the expiration of our present commitments—that is, in 1969 at the latest—the subordination known as integration, which is provided for by NATO, which hands our fate over to foreign authority, shall cease." But the integrated command was not a commitment of the North Atlantic Treaty, and de Gaulle felt free to move up his deadline—at least partly, I should think, because of the growing threat that the Vietnam war would spread. On February 21, 1966, he announced that he was "reestablishing a normal situation of sovereignty in which that which is French, as regards land, sky, sea, and [armed] forces, will in the future be under French command alone." The United States, which appears to have been given private warning well before that, of course declined to place its forces under French command,

and the deadline of March 31, 1967, for our departure followed.

It is interesting to consider how we might have behaved if the situation were reversed and if, say, a French army had remained in the United States for a generation after the War of Independence, to protect us against the British, with its own French command and power of decision as to its use. I suspect that our Founding Fathers would have agreed with Premier Pompidou, who asked in the National Assembly, "How can it be imagined that this might become for decades, if not for generations, the normal international status for a country such as ours?"

The reproach that de Gaulle should have given us time to negotiate a reform is absurd, not merely because he did give us time, but because the fundamental issue was not negotiable. There has never been any question of our giving anyone else the power to order our nuclear force into action, or to veto it. As Walter Lippmann commented after the Cuban missile showdown of 1962, this awful power "cannot be divided or shared"; it is like a car speeding on a hairpin mountain road—"only one man can sit at the wheel." This was tolerable to most West Europeans, as long as we drove carefully. But a series of crises in other parts of the world—especially the Dominican occupation and the Vietnam war—have caused growing doubts about our cool-headedness. These doubts were reinforced by Barry Goldwater's prayer in 1964 that China would give us a pretext to bomb her. They were allayed by Goldwater's overwhelming defeat, but Europeans were as dismayed as were liberal Americans to see Johnson adopting Goldwater's line. Whether hawks or doves, most Americans, according to Gallup, now believe that our involvement in Vietnam was a blunder. We should be big enough to admit, then, that on this issue Johnson should have heeded de Gaulle rather than Goldwater. In January, 1964, when Johnson had been President for only two months and all we had in Vietnam were "counselors," de Gaulle recognized Peking, explaining that the troubles in Indochina could only be solved by neutralizing the region, and that this could only be achieved with the consent of China. (Rusk replied that a neutral Indochina would in fact be a Communist Indochina.) De Gaulle foresaw the tragedy that was coming, did what he could to avert it, and put himself in a position to help both sides find a relatively painless and dignified exit. But once again, de Gaulle was right too soon; if Americans remember his act of statesmanship, they remember it as another Gaullist stab in the back.

## The force de frappe

Many Frenchmen raise a strong argument against de Gaulle's atomic armament: the moral one. To moralists the use of nuclear weapons is unthinkable because by their nature they are instruments of genocide. But we Americans are hardly in a position to take this stance, so our objections are materialistic: The *force de frappe* is an absurdly ineffectual, terribly costly bauble that de Gaulle in his vanity seeks for the adornment of poor little France; it is also a constant incitement to other little countries, such as Germany, to do likewise. For Americans, this argument is better than the moral one, but not much.

As it happens, the French began developing their atomic bomb under the Fourth Republic, not the Fifth, although it was de Gaulle who pushed the work to completion and ordered the planes, rockets, and submarines necessary to deliver such a weapon. In May, 1962, we turned down his request that we sell him such essential elements as equipment for the processing of uranium ore, blueprints for nuclear submarines, and guidance systems and fuel for rockets. Later, we blocked the sale of large computers. Our refusal is certainly defensible; it would have been more effective, perhaps, if it had been accompanied by serious progress toward nuclear disarmament. We did offer France Polaris missiles, on condition that we keep control of the warheads. De Gaulle wouldn't take them. He went ahead to develop his own atomic force, from the ground up. This was indeed expensive, as the Opposition in France often pointed out. The government replied that the cost was offset by a reduction in conventional forces, so that France's military budget was about the same as those of Britain and West Germany, and also that the development of advanced technology in chemistry, metallurgy, and electronics was a valuable "fallout" of the *force de frappe.* There is something to be said for both sides of this debate, but it does not really concern us as Americans, except to the degree that we confront the same problem in the allocation of our resources. So far we have made the same choice as has France, but on a much larger scale.

It is flattering to our vanity to say that the *force de frappe* is a popgun, so journalists doubling as strategists frequently say so. Our experts do not. They have kept a close eye on de Gaulle's weapons development, as illustrated by the embarrassing flight of an American photo reconnaissance plane over the Pierrelatte uranium plant in July, 1965. I may say from personal conversations that American specialists have a very high regard for French military missile technology; this is shared by the military authorities of many countries, including Israel, which have bought French rockets. A respectful assessment of the *force de frappe* was published in 1967 by the authoritative Institute for Strategic Studies. It was written by an American analyst, Judith H. Young of the Brown & Shaw Research Corporation, one of the "think tanks" often employed by the Pentagon. (It represents a curious sort of progress, I suppose, that women may now advise generals on the technology of megadeaths.) Mrs. Young was on the whole admiring of what the French had accomplished. She estimated that, had it not been for our refusal to cooperate, France would have deployed strategic missiles four or five years earlier. But the resulting necessity to work out the basic problems, she said, "has given France a capability and independence she might not otherwise have possessed, particularly with regard to further exports of missile technology." She concluded, "Consequently, it would be useful to examine further the granting of licenses, under some circumstances, as a possible means of controlling the secondary diffusion of critical technologies." In other words, it might be better for the United States to supply the answers than for other countries to develop basic technology. This fairly coldblooded thesis goes far toward conceding the Gaullist (and prevailing American) argument that the development of nuclear war technology is a good thing in itself. Many people will not be persuaded, however. They will continue to feel that the main result of the spread of nuclear weapons is to multiply the threat of a nuclear holocaust, and they will reproach de Gaulle for resisting a nonproliferation treaty. His reply is that nonproliferation is not disarmament but maintenance of the status quo. He says no country able to give itself nuclear weapons will forever deprive itself of such defense while the United States, the Soviet Union, Britain, and China have them. He proposes instead a ban on nuclear weapons— a proposal that still is premature, in the view of Americans.

Most Americans, I suppose, think it silly of France to spend billions on a deterrent when the United States maintains one for free. But the credibility of our deterrent has declined with the growth of Chinese deterrents. This was vividly demonstrated quite recently when the United States decided to build an antimissile umbrella, comparable to one allegedly being raised by the Soviet Union. Europeans asked immediately a question that did not seem to have occurred to the American planners: What about an umbrella for *them?* NATO studied it, then dropped it as too expensive and ineffectual. It seemed a confirmation of de Gaulle's warning years earlier that the United States could not guarantee France against destruction. "For France to deny herself her own means of deterring the adversary," he said, "would be to attract the lightning while depriving herself of a lightning rod."

There remains a large question about the credibility of de Gaulle's deterrent. Among those who like to play the parlor game of Armageddon, a large number hold that the aggressor would take out the French deterrent in a matter of minutes. The French reply that if only one of their missile submarines-to-be, or only one of their "hardened" missile silos escapes the first attack, the enemy will lose a metropolis, or two or three. That's a high-enough price, they say, to deter any aggressor from attacking a country that is not looking for trouble.

Now, all these war games naturally assume that the Soviet Union would be the aggressor (although de Gaulle has lately raised a few eyebrows with his talk of a defense *tout azimuths* —that is, able to retaliate in *any direction*). But whether the *force de frappe* does or does not render France safe against attack from a great nuclear power, there can be little question that it renders her safe from a power that *doesn't have any atom bombs.*

Such a power is Germany.

Granted, the idea of a fourth German invasion of France is fantastic. Surely, the holocaust of 1941–45 put martial ambition out of the German mind forever (in spite of Lehrer's bitter line, "We taught them a lesson in 1918, and they've hardly bothered us since then"). But we cannot expect former victims of the Reich to be as cool headed on the subject as we are. Their bitter memories are continually being stirred up. The cold war nipped denazification in the bud, and we have learned to make do with Germans more or less tainted by the Hitler era, but many Europeans feel uneasy about the pasts of Germany's present civilian and military leaders, about their refusal to recognize Germany's postwar frontiers, and about the recent upsurge of neo-Nazism. This uneasiness gives point to a probably apocryphal story: De Gaulle's military experts were discussing with him their plans for an intercontinental ballistic missile. "Why," he demanded, "do we need an ICBM to hit Düsseldorf?"

As far as I can tell, President de Gaulle has never so much as hinted in public that there was such a thing as a German threat. But he himself fought the Germans in two wars; in between, he made himself rather a nuisance in military-political circles with his demands for armor to meet the next German attack. One may doubt that he has ever abandoned this concern.

In light of the record, it is absurd to accuse the French of inciting the Germans to obtain atomic weapons. A preoccupation of the United States since the war has been to strengthen West Germany's defenses; a preoccupation of French policy has been to keep us from strengthening them too much. As a result we have found ourselves in the grotesque situation of rivals for the hand of our former common foe.

We have offered wealth and weapons, including a share of the nuclear deterrent. De Gaulle has offered independence in a Franco-German alliance. Both wooers have also held out hope for an ultimate reunification of Germany, the Americans by way of a tough line toward the Russians, the French by way of a *détente*. Cynics have wondered whether either was sincere. Some have gone so far as to wonder whether Bonn was always as anxious for reunification as it claimed to be; the hard line has been followed now for twenty-odd years, and all it has brought the Germans is the Berlin Wall. De Gaulle, on the other hand, has urged the Germans to take the opposite tack: Loosen their close tie to United States policy, recognize the Oder-Neisse line, and build bridges toward the East.

This is in fact a basic dispute between the United States and France. Ambassador Bohlen summed it up in a speech before his departure from Paris in early 1968: We do not believe, he said, that there has been any fundamental change in the nature of the Soviet menace that would warrant our lowering our guard. Well, how fundamental must the changes be? Our cold-war line was developed to confront a Communist monolith. Since then, Moscow and Peking have split, and Yugoslavia, Albania, Rumania, Hungary, Poland, and Czechoslovakia have established their independence in varying degrees. Washington hawks may insist that these more or less agreeable developments are a *result* of our firmness, but the available evidence suggests that fear of the United States (and, in Europe, fear of our German ally) has been the strongest remaining link among members of the Communist bloc. Our intervention in Vietnam, which forces Moscow and Peking to preserve a snarling alliance, is an outstanding example.

If in fact there has been a change in the Soviet menace, it would seem to call for a basic review of the structure of NATO, which was designed in the Stalinist epoch. This, as Bohlen implied, we refuse to do. Events have confirmed the French declaration of March 12, 1966, that negotiations to reform NATO would have been doomed to failure, since the partners of France appear to be, or say they are, all partisans of the maintenance of the status quo. But there were a few dissenters among us. Twenty-one Republican congressmen signed a declaration charging that the Administration had helped to "delay the constructive evolution of NATO" by putting all the blame on de Gaulle, and the Senate Majority Leader, Mike Mansfield, commented that de Gaulle had given us plenty of warning and had even "performed a needed service" in forcing changes in NATO, which might lead to reducing American forces in Europe. But the Administration proclaimed at every occasion that it had no intention of either reforming NATO or reducing our forces in Europe.

We often accuse de Gaulle of blind obstinacy, but it is difficult to find other words to characterize Washington's position. We had apparently elected to become the gendarmes of the whole world, but were not prepared to pay the price, which would be full wartime mobilization. Short of this, we could not satisfy General Westmoreland's demands for troops in Vietnam. Yet we refused to accept the golden opportunity offered us by de Gaulle to trim our commitments in Europe. The cold warriors were afraid that a cutback would encourage "our" Germans to strike a deal with the Reds. Our hawks are easily frightened. They tremble at the threats of every client dictator to leave our bed and board. These threats have about as much substance as the brags of the China lobby about what Chiang Kai-shek would do if only we would unleash him.

It would in fact be to our best interest if "our" Germans abandoned their claims to territory lost during World War II, and sought a modus vivendi with their Eastern neighbors. The current of history is running in that direction, anyhow. When that day arrives, the rival blocs should be able to lighten their military burdens and turn their full energies to the world's most urgent problem, alleviating poverty. Then it would appear that de Gaulle had been a prophet. I'm afraid we shall never forgive him for it.

# 7

# DE GAULLE AND CANADA

> CANDIDE. *You know England; are they as mad there as in France?*
> MARTIN. *It's another kind of madness. You know these two countries are at war about a few acres of snow, over Canada way, and they're spending much more on that fine war than Canada's worth. To tell you exactly whether there are more people fit to be tied in the one country than in the other, is more than my feeble glimmerings would allow me.*
>
> —*Voltaire*

CHARLES DE GAULLE is, let's face it, a shocking man. He was never more so, perhaps, than on July 24, 1967, when he raised his arms in Montreal and cried, "*Vive le Québec libre!*". Even his partisans at home were reduced to stunned silence. When the Prime Minister of Canada rather mildly observed that such behavior by a visiting chief of state was "unacceptable," I reported from Paris: "President de Gaulle flew home tonight to an embarrassed and bewildered nation." The press openly asked whether the "Canadian fiasco" was not a "paroxysm of a senile man's anti-American obsession." Two distinguished American journalists of my acquaintance consulted a specialist to determine whether the old man was not indeed falling into the last stages of dotage. (To their disappointment, the doctor said de Gaulle showed no signs of it; in fact, he looked great.)

What the French press, my American colleagues, and, I must admit, I myself had forgotten was that de Gaulle had always been like that. This is easy to forget because so many things de Gaulle does that are shocking at the time seem less shocking in retrospect. He shocked the brass when, in the thirties, he carried on like a Gallic Billy Mitchell about the need for mobile armor to meet a coming German attack. He shocked them again when, in June, 1940, he refused to acknowledge their armistice and set himself up as the legitimate spokesman for France—in defiance of his own mentor, the national hero Marshal Pétain, who then had the blessing of his church and of the overwhelming majority of his people. Through the war he shocked the Allies by his insubordination, from St. Pierre and Miquelon in 1941 to Strasbourg in 1944. When the politicians of the Fourth Republic refused to abandon their intrigues in favor of his vision of France, he shocked them—though not enough—by stalking off into exile at Colombey-les-Deux-Églises. When a decade later they appealed to him to save the Republic, he shocked democratic opinion by taking over with a ruthless disregard for law and recasting the constitution to give France a strong executive branch. (Many liberals have still not forgiven him for it, but hardly anybody in France now wants to return to the revolving "*combines*" of the Fourth Republic.) With shocking duplicity, he told the insurgent generals and European settlers in Algeria, "I have understood you," while he prepared to make peace and bring them to heel. Disdaining their bombings and their attempts on his life, he demanded that the world accept France as a great and independent power, equal in rights, wisdom, and virtue to those two "colossi," the United

States and the Soviet Union. It is now rather the fashion in Europe to deplore the trend toward economic colonization by the United States, to criticize our monetary policy, and to decry our behavior in Vietnam, but when de Gaulle first uttered such heresies, they sent tremors across the continents. In short, a shocking man.

The tactic is deliberate. De Gaulle is quoted as having told intimates, "I did not become chief of state to inaugurate chrysanthemums." Whether he said it or not, it is a fair description of his behavior. I am not myself an enthusiast of this *weltpolitik*, but then I am not a statesman. Sad to report, there is a quality of ruthlessness about even the most admirable of great men—Lincoln, Roosevelt, La Guardia—without which they could never have left their mark. And there can be no doubt about de Gaulle's leaving his mark. Not long ago an Anglo-Canadian reporter told me: "There can be no denying that de Gaulle's trip last year brought attention to a situation that needed it. When he first visited Canada in 1960, he behaved himself; it was so boring he nearly fell asleep on the platform. Who remembers that visit now? But after 1967 . . ."

If there was indeed a situation that needed attention, history must certainly award a large share of the blame to France. De Gaulle has accused his country of having neglected Canada for two centuries. It is an understatement. France neglected Canada from the first settlement, four and a half centuries ago. The colony was left under the tight rule of soldier-aristocrats and Jesuit missionaries; while the Age of Enlightenment was flourishing in the homeland, not a glimmer seems to have reached Canada. It is a shocking fact that the first printing press was admitted only after Wolfe defeated Montcalm on the Plains of Abraham in 1759. Voltaire's dismissal of Canada as "not worth the bones of a grenadier" was translated into France's decision at the peace conference that followed to abandon the "few acres of snow" to the British, in favor of recovering Martinique and Guadeloupe. If Quebec has since remained more backward than English-speaking Canada, surely that is in part a product of its French heritage. But to say this does not resolve the problem.

Canada is today an economic dependency of the United States. An OECD survey in 1968, citing five-year-old figures, said U.S. interests controlled 46 percent of its manufacturing, 52 percent of its mining, and 62 percent of its oil production, not to mention two thirds of its foreign trade. The proportions today are evidently much higher. "In these conditions," the OECD observed, "the business climate and the rhythm of economic life in Canada are necessarily strongly influenced by trends in the United States, and it is sometimes difficult for Canadian policy to overcome these influences." Another result, it should be pointed out, is that the Canadian standard of living approaches that of the United States, on average. But the standard is visibly lower in Quebec than in English-speaking Canada. And the control of industry in the province by English-speaking interests—U.S., British, or Anglo-Canadian—runs to such proportions as 95 percent of mining, 93 percent of banking and so on. So that, if all Canada is now pondering how to preserve its integrity, French-speaking Canada confronts a far more agonizing problem—the total loss of its identity.

As long as Quebec was a province of poor farmers, trappers, and lumberjacks, the preservation of its language and culture —such as it was—presented no particular problem. But the postwar industrial revolution put a hard choice to growing numbers of young French-Canadians: Speak English, or accept a lowly status in their own country. (Even *speaking* English, of course, did not guarantee equality.) "We felt inferior," an intellectual from Montreal told me not long ago. "Our psychology was that, to succeed, we had to learn English, think English, dress English. For social standing, a degree from Oxford was the thing." In technology and business, an American degree was the thing. Quebec was on the road to assimilation, the road Louisiana had taken long before.

We Anglos may regard such a development with complacency, if we bother thinking about it at all. But to many young *Québecois*, the prospect was intolerable. First, a handful of extremists shocked their elders with bombings of English monuments. Then, around 1960, something more important developed, out of sight and out of mind of the American and even the French public. This is what is now known as the Quiet Revolution. Forward-looking French Canadians took over the destiny of Quebec for the first time in its history. They ousted the province's old political bosses, who were among the most reactionary on the continent, and began to modernize the primitive school system, which until then had been left entirely to the Church. Inevitably, the Quiet Revolution turned toward France. Only France had the textbooks and the teachers it needed, the literature and culture it demanded; only in France could a youth learn engineering or the sciences—in French. Students, who a few years ago would have gone to Toronto, Boston, or London, now went to Paris instead. A decade ago, almost the only Canadians in France were a few pensioners. Today, there are several thousand students, writers, and actors stocking up on French culture and know-how. The change in their attitudes, as they recount it, has been dramatic. Until recently, French-Canadians harbored a feeling of resentment toward the *patrie* that had abandoned them. Now, as I was told by a Canadian diplomat who is firmly opposed to French foreign policy, "De Gaulle has rebuilt a France that Quebec is proud of."

There can be no doubt that the Quiet Revolution took some of its inspiration from Gaullist France. But France did not *incite* the revolution. It was the new leaders of Quebec who came to Paris, seeking help. "Franco-Québecois cooperation is our only chance of survival," said Premier Daniel Johnson (who despite his name is, of course, a French-Canadian).

Most of the French, it must be said, could not have cared less. To them Canada was an embarrassing episode from their past, a "few acres of snow" inhabited by a backward people with a funny accent, and now another candidate for French foreign aid. The French taxpayer takes little pride in the fact that he spends more to help foreign countries than any other taxpayer in the world. But de Gaulle heeded the plea of Quebec with an enthusiasm that grew to alarming proportions. There could be no objection to his grant of cultural aid—teacher exchanges and the like. But by the spring of 1967 de Gaulle was according Premier Johnson the honors of a visiting chief of state, and toasting him with the words, "All Frenchmen, wherever they come from and wherever they are, are now profoundly convinced of the great destiny that is common to them." *Le Monde* nervously asked that he "define this 'great common destiny' as rapidly as possible, to avoid all misunderstanding and false hopes." Johnson had invited de Gaulle to visit Quebec, and *Le Monde* prayed that he would not "throw oil on the fire." Its prayer was not answered.

De Gaulle's behavior in Quebec could scarcely be defended by anybody but, perhaps, a French-Canadian. It was not defended, at the time, by most of the French. From right to left, the press decried his "unheard of brutality," his "grave discourtesy," his "imprudence," his "anti-American phobia," his "senility." (This in a country often described abroad as a dictatorship!) The Communist daily *L'Humanité* felt impelled to call for "noninterference in the internal affairs of foreign states." (The only discordance in the press chorus came, curiously, from the French newsmen accompanying de Gaulle, who seemed to have been carried away by the enthusiasm of the crowds. Their dispatches contrasted oddly with the editorials in their papers. They joined their Quebec colleagues in a resolution of complaint about the coverage of the event in the English-language press. Not having been there, I cannot judge the merit of their charges.)

The first reaction of the public seemed to be the same as that of the editorialists. In a movie house on the Champs-Elysées, a newsreel shot of de Gaulle in Quebec was greeted with cries of "Shame!" A cabinet minister was quoted as having told intimates that the general had been "a little gross." The affair, following de Gaulle's unpopular stand on the Israeli war, emboldened his restive political ally, Giscard d'Estaing, to take public issue with the general's "solitary exercise of power." To outsiders, it seemed as if the government was about to fall.

In Montreal, de Gaulle dismissed the uproar with one of his famous phrases: *"Tout ce qui grouille, grenouille, scribouille n'a pas de consequence historique."* ("All this wriggling, squiggling, and scribbling is of no historic consequence.") He arrived back at Orly airport evidently still uplifted by his reception in Canada and altogether satisfied with himself. He seems to have been genuinely shocked to find that not all France shared his elation. He quickly rallied his spokesmen from their stupefaction to a strong defense, and while some

bemused newsmen were predicting that he would apologize
to Ottawa, he escalated. He protested that French-Canadians
did not enjoy "liberty, equality, and fraternity," and promised
that France would "help them reach the objectives of libera-
tion that they themselves have set." To complaints of interference he replied that France "most certainly cannot dis-
interest herself in the present and future fate of a people de-
scended from her own people, and admirably faithful to their
country of origin, nor consider Canada as a foreign country,
in the same sense as others." Finally, at his November 27 news
conference, he predicted that Quebec would become "a sovereign state."

Whatever one may think of his conduct, there can be no
question about his sincerity. Certainly none will question it
who attended that conference. There he touched on all the
big questions of domestic and foreign policy in a manner al-
ternately lofty and earthy, humorous and grave, but he was
deeply emotional, even exalted, only when he spoke of the
Canadian "miracle," the "magnificent" fecundity of a people
who multiplied and survived, and who greeted him on "the
king's road" from Quebec to Montreal with an "immense
wave of French faith and hope." He read a passage by the
poet Paul Valéry terming the survival of French Canada an
inspiration to the homeland, and chiding the French for their
ignorance of Canada. De Gaulle concluded, "Ah! What would
he have said of our press, had he lived long enough to read
what so many, many of our newspapers have published—have
they not?—on the occasion of the visit paid by General de
Gaulle to the French people of Canada? Come, come! For
them too, for them above all, France must be France."

An earlier passage touched on a vital element in de Gaulle's
policy: "Whether the French language wins or loses the bat-

tle will weigh heavily in the struggle that is being waged for it from one end of the world to the other." There are those who believe that this preoccupation is one reason for de Gaulle's veto of British entry into the Common Market—the likelihood that English would oust French as the dominant language in the market's administration, as it has in diplomacy and the business world. France under de Gaulle is waging a fight for the preservation and diffusion of her language that is surely unique. She maintains 32,000 teachers abroad and educates tens of thousands of foreign teachers in France; she sponsors all kinds of institutions linking the thirty-two "francophone" countries. Her delegation to the United Nations has campaigned for equal status for French in workday operations, where English has steadily forged ahead. The fact that a Romanian delegate addressed the U.N. Assembly in French was remarked upon with pride by Foreign Minister Couve de Murville. (Pride in French is not a Gaullist invention, of course. Tradition has it that at the Versailles Conference when Lloyd George said "Yes" or "No," Clemenceau would blandly order, "Translation!") On this issue, de Gaulle is hard to challenge on his home ground; and even abroad, many people would be sorry to see the world and all its rich diversity of cultures homogenized into a single culture with a single language.

De Gaulle's domestic critics made headway when they questioned his manners, but got poor scores when they questioned his consistency and his courage. If Quebec should be free, they asked, why not Brittany or Provence? The Gaullists shrugged that aside as irrelevant and absurd; all three places are French, they'd say, and none can survive without France. The opposition jibed: If de Gaulle dared cry, "*Vive le Québec libre!*" in Montreal, then let him cry "*Vive la Pologne libre!*"

in Warsaw. The jest vanished the day de Gaulle did just that. He told his Polish hosts that both their countries must "safeguard their substance, their influence, and their national power, whatever be the weight of the colossi of the universe." His critics hastily shifted ground, complaining now that de Gaulle had sacrificed his own policy of bringing East and West together, without persuading the Poles to be free. (It is a measure of de Gaulle's stature that he is frequently accused of not working miracles.) Back in Paris, the general replied, "To encourage Poland to be herself is not to renounce Soviet friendship; to recognize the frontier resulting from the war and to encourage Poland to reach an understanding with her neighbors is not to renounce German friendship; to want a Europe master of itself and to deplore the Vietnamese war is not to renounce American friendship."

Is de Gaulle's interference in Canada another cause for Americans to renounce French friendship? In light of our own recent conduct in a number of countries, we are hardly in the best position to deplore intervention on principle. We may take a neighborly—even a proprietary—interest in the fate of Canada, but it is by no means clear what kind of Canada our interest requires. A secure and reasonably happy Canada, certainly, but not necessarily a monolithic one.

Many Anglo-Canadians now concede that de Gaulle brought a blaze of attention to a situation they themselves had neglected, and some even think he may have speeded a solution. Once again it would be wise, before passing judgment on de Gaulle, to await the verdict of history.

# 8

## AFTER DE GAULLE

*"Rest assured, I shall not fail to die, some day."*
*—de Gaulle at a news conference, replying to a question about his health.*

A SURPRISING NUMBER of people seem to think that the planets will slip back into orbit when de Gaulle departs. He is so obviously one of those men who shift the course of history that they think history would not have moved without him. But with or without great men, it moves. Tito may have advanced by a few years the progress of the Soviet satellites toward independence; it now seems (from hindsight, to be sure) hardly likely that this movement could long have been delayed. It is tempting, if hackneyed, to suggest that if there had not been a Tito, Eastern Europe would have had to invent one. If there had not been a de Gaulle . . .

Well, France might have found a Mendès, but Mendès was not de Gaulle. Without de Gaulle, the country probably would have remained in a dreadful mess, and Western Europe with it. France almost certainly would have stayed in NATO (as Greece has stayed), but it is hard to see what difference that would make, except that GI wives would still be getting their hair done at the PX in Belle Manoir, and the officers' club on Rue Marbeuf would still be serving fifteen-cent martinis during the Happy Hour.

Without de Gaulle, the French Government would probably not have denounced our policy in Vietnam, and the first peace negotiations would probably not have been held in Paris. Israel would still have conquered the Arabs in six days and would still be at war with them, but the Arabs would be firmly convinced that they had no friend in the West.

Without de Gaulle, the Common Market, if it survived France's internal troubles, would probably have begun negotiations with Britain. But if the negotiations succeeded—which is by no means certain—it would no longer have been a common market. It would be a free-trade area, even less able than the Common Market to resist the pressures of national interest. Sooner or later, France or some other member would find it necessary to put up the barriers again.

Without de Gaulle, the world monetary system would have undergone a crisis, perhaps a little later, more likely a good deal sooner. France, as well as Britain, might well have been a "sick man of Europe," and the collapse of the franc might well have preceded the fall of sterling. Otherwise, France would probably have remained in the London Gold Pool until it broke up, but it is quite possible that, like Italy and Switzerland, she would have surreptitiously bought gold from the United States to replace the gold she was selling in London. The United States would have continued to run a huge payments deficit—an even larger one, if we had to shore up the franc as well as the pound—our European creditors would have continued to grumble, and the dollar would have continued to head for a fall.

"Eh bien," de Gaulle said, "everyone comes to an end. . . . 'After de Gaulle' may happen this evening, or in six months, or in a year. . . . If I wanted to make a few people laugh, or others groan, I would say that it could equally well take another ten or fifteen years. Frankly, I do not think so."

Eh bien, all we can say with any certainty is that the world, after de Gaulle, will not be the same as it was before. De Gaulle's helpers may survive his departure or may be succeeded by a Popular Front regime or, perhaps more likely, a coalition of moderate conservatives and liberals may take over, as in much of Western Europe. But it will not in any case be the same France as before de Gaulle. Even if some of the ministers are the same as before, they will not restore the Fourth Republic, they will not revive the empire and reconquer Algeria, and they will not invite us to station troops in France again.

And it is hardly likely that we would want to come back! For we, too, have changed, and so has the world.

Since World War II, our policy has been dominated by a single goal, the containment of Communism. Now, we are dimly becoming aware that the No. One problem in the world is not the cleavage between Us and Them, but between the Rich and the Poor. It is increasingly evident that the cold war and NATO are irrelevant to this problem—or rather are an active handicap to its solution.

If we have learned anything from our recent tribulations, it is that we cannot solve everything by ourselves. In fact, there is no simple solution, but even to make a beginning we need all the help we can get. In this effort we are fortunate, even if we do not fully appreciate it, in having as an ally a prosperous, stable and independent France, actively concerned with the Third World.

Thanks to de Gaulle.

# APPENDIX

## De Gaulle on French Nuclear Policy
## and the Nassau Agreement
## (Press Conference of January 14, 1963)

I repeat, after having said it so often, that France intends to have her own national defense. It is obvious that one country, especially one such as ours, cannot in the present day and age . . . conduct a major modern war all by itself. To have allies goes without saying for us in the historic period we are in. But also for a great people to have the free disposition of itself and the means to struggle to preserve it is an absolute imperative, for alliances have no absolute virtues, whatever may be the sentiments on which they are based. . . . We are in the atomic age, and we are a country that can be destroyed at any moment unless the aggressor is deterred from the undertaking by the certainty that he too will suffer frightful destruction. This justifies both alliance and independence. . . . The Americans, finding themselves exposed to a direct atomic attack from the Caribbean, acted in such a way as to rid themselves of that menace and, if it had been necessary, to crush it *without its having occurred to them or to anyone else that the game would necessarily be played in Europe and without recourse to the direct assistance of the Europeans.* Moreover, the means which they immediately decided to employ in order to counter a direct attack, whether it came from Cuba only or was combined with another originating elsewhere, these means were automatically set aside for something other than the defense of Europe, even if Europe had been attacked in its turn. And then, above and beyond everything, the deterrent is now a fact for the Russians as for the Americans, which means that in the case of a general atomic war, there would inevitably be frightful and perhaps fatal destruction in both countries. In these conditions, no one in the world—particularly no one in America—can say if, where, when, how, and to what extent the American nuclear weapons would be employed to defend Europe. . . . Moreover, this does not in the least prevent the American nuclear weapons, which are the most powerful of all, from remaining the essential guarantee of world peace. This fact, and the determination with which President Kennedy used it, came into full light out of the Cuban affair. But it remains that the American nuclear power does not necessarily and immediately meet all eventualities concerning Europe and France.

Thus, principles and realities combine to lead France to equip itself with an atomic force of its own. This does not at all exclude, of course, the combination of the action of this force with the action of the similar forces of its allies. But, for us, in this specific case, integration is something that is unimaginable. . . . It is completely understandable that this French [nuclear] undertaking does not appear to be highly satisfactory to certain American circles. In politics and in strategy, as in the economy, monopoly quite naturally appears to the person who holds it to be the best possible system. . . .

It is quite true that the number of nuclear weapons with which we can equip ourselves will not equal, far from it, the mass of those of the two giants of today. . . . I only want to say that the French atomic force . . . will have the somber and terrible capability of destroying in a few seconds millions and millions of men. This fact cannot fail to have at least some bearing on the intents of any possible aggressor. . . .

France has taken note of the Anglo-American Nassau agreement. As it was conceived, undoubtedly no one will be surprised that we cannot subscribe to it. It truly would not be useful for us to buy Polaris missiles when we have neither the submarines to launch them nor the thermonuclear warheads to arm them. . . . In terms of technology, this affair is not the question of the moment. But also, it does not meet with the principle about which I just spoke and which consists of disposing in our own right of our deterrent force. To turn over our weapons to a multilateral force, under a foreign command, would be to act contrary to that principle of our defense and our policy. It is true that we too can theoretically retain the ability to take back in our hands, in the supreme hypothesis, our atomic weapons incorporated in the multilateral force. But how could we do it in practice during the unheard of moments of the atomic apocalypse? And then, this multilateral force necessarily entails a web of liaisons, transmissions, and interferences within itself, and on the outside a ring of obligations such that, if an integral part were suddenly snatched from it, there would be a strong risk of paralyzing it just at the moment . . . when it should act.

In sum, we will adhere to the decision we have made: to construct and, if necessary, to employ our atomic force ourselves. And that without refusing, of course, cooperation, be it technological or strategic, if this cooperation is, on the other hand, desired by our allies.

## Couve de Murville on Self-Defense
### (Press Conference of October 29, 1963)

Foreign Minister Maurice Couve de Murville in the National Assembly, Oct. 29, 1963: The United States has been complaining for years now that the Europe of today, risen again from the ruins of the war, is not making a big-enough effort for its own defense, leaving the United States with the main part of the burden, as in the distant days of 1950 when it alone possessed the necessary resources. And, in fact, most of its European allies find quite convenient a situation in which they can thus, without other preoccupations, attend to their own affairs. . . . That is why France wanted to get back control of her own forces—whether of the army, navy, or the air force. That is why she decided on a military atomic program of her own. In doing this she may have upset some of the fixed ideas in the Atlantic alliance. But she has shown herself as having a national will, and as a result is a real ally. The day when necessary changes are made and other European members of the alliance show the same will, then a reorganization of the Atlantic alliance on durable foundations will become possible. Then we can satisfy America's legitimate request for a different distribution of duties, because there will be a different distribution of responsibilities. Then we will assure the maintenance of this alliance and consequently the participation of the United States in the defense of Europe. . . . Systematic agreement is not a policy. Nor is it, in an alliance, a guarantee of commitments made. France is perhaps a difficult ally. She is above all a loyal and sure ally in a serious crisis, and everyone can testify to this.

## De Gaulle on Gold

De Gaulle's first comprehensive statement on gold came at his press conference of February 4, 1965:

Insofar as the nations of Europe—which were ruined and decimated by the wars—are recovering their substance, their relative position tends to appear inadequate and even, frequently, abusive and dangerous. [There is] incidentally nothing in these observations implying on their part—and *a fortiori* on France's part—anything inamicable with regard to any country, and in particular with regard to the United States; but the fact that those [European] countries wish more and more every day to act on their own in all fields of international relations proceeds from the natural movement of things. It is thus with the monetary system which is practiced, with monetary relations, if you will, which have been in force in the world ever since the trials she underwent made Europe lose equilibrium. I want, of course, to refer to the international monetary system which made its appearance immediately after the First World War and which established itself following the second. It is known that this system came out of the Geneva conference. This system attributed to two currencies, the Pound and the Dollar, the privilege of being considered as equivalents of gold in external exchanges. It is true that the Pound was devalued in 1931 and the Dollar in 1933, and one could have thought at the time that the privilege, this outstanding advantage for those two currencies, was compromised. But America surmounted its big crisis, and soon after, the Second World War ruined the currencies of Western Europe by unleashing inflation.

Since furthermore almost all of the world's gold reserves were then held by the United States and since they were the universal supplier and, consequently, able to maintain the value of their currency, it could seem natural that countries would indifferently let dollars or gold enter their exchange reserves and that differences in the balances of payments should be settled through the transfer of the credits or the American monetary symbols as well as through the precious metal; all the more so as America would have no difficulty in settling her debts in gold were this asked of her. And this international monetary system, this Gold Exchange Standard, has consequently been admitted as a practice ever since.

But it so happens that it no more corresponds in the same way to the realities in the present and that, consequently, it brings about disadvantages which are increasingly heavy to bear. As this question—which is of interest to everybody—must be considered with serenity and objectivity (which the present juncture permits since, in this respect, it involves nothing that appears either very pressing or very alarming) this is the moment to do so.

Let us observe that the conditions which had given rise to the Gold Exchange Standard have changed profoundly. The currencies of Western Europe have been restored to such a point that the gold reserves which these countries possess, let us say, these six countries, the Six, that the total of their gold reserves is equivalent to that of the Americans, and that it would even surpass it if these countries wished to convert into gold all the dollars they have in their accounts. So, the kind of transcendent value recognized for the dollar has lost its initial basis, which was America's possession of the world's gold.

But beyond that, the fact that many countries accept Dollars on principle, just as they would gold, for the settlement of disparities existing in their favor in the American balance of payments—this fact leads the Americans to indebting themselves gratuitously abroad. This is because what they owe they pay—at least partly—with Dollars, which it is up to them to issue, and not with gold, which has a real value, which only he possesses who has earned it, which one cannot transfer to others without risk and without sacrifice. But at the same time, this sort of unilateral facility which was attributed to America contributes to dispel the idea according to which the Dollar is an impartial and international symbol of exchange—when it is a means of credit appropriate for one country.

Evidently, there are other consequences from this situation: in particular, the fact that the United States—not being obliged to settle the negative disparities in their payments in gold, at least not entirely (contrary to the practices adopted at the time and by virtue of which the United States were impelled to take, and rigorously evaluate, the measures necessary for establishing their equilibrium, if the case arose)—suffer year in year out from a deficit balance. It is not that the aggregate of their commercial exchanges be in their disfavor. On the contrary, their exports of products always exceed their imports. But this is also the case for the Dollars the outflow of which always exceeds the inflow. In other words, by means which one is forced to call inflation capital is created in America which, in the form of Dollar loans granted to countries or individuals, is exported abroad. Since in the very United States the increase in fiduciary circulation which results from this in turn makes internal investment less remunerative, a growing tendency appears there to invest abroad.

From there stems, for certain countries, a kind of expropriation of this or that among their enterprises. One has to say that this practice long has furthered and to a certain degree still is furthering the multiple and considerable aid which America gives to many countries and from which we ourselves have greatly benefited in other times. But the circumstances have changed. And this is why France advocates that the system, too, be changed, that an end be put to this kind of fundamental disequilibrium which as of now is a fact. France called for this, as you know, at the Tokyo monetary conference. In view of the consequences which a crisis could have in such a field, we believe that measures to avoid it should be taken in time. We consider it necessary that international exchanges be established—as was the case before the great calamities in the world—on an indisputable monetary basis and which bears the mark of no country in particular.

Which basis? In truth, one does not see that there could really be a criterion, a standard, other than gold. Well, indeed: gold, which does not change its nature, which can be indifferently cast as ingot, bar, or as coins, which has no nationality, which is perennially and universally taken for the inalterable credit value par excellence. And, for the rest, whatever in the middle of the immense trials that we have all gone through one may have imagined or said, or written, or done, the fact is that to this day no currency has value except through direct or indirect, real or supposed relation to gold. Naturally, one cannot force any country to do what it must do inside of itself. But in international exchanges, the supreme law, the golden rule—as indeed one can say here— which one must reinstate and reenforce is the obligation to equilibrate from one monetary zone to the other through effective entry and exit of precious metal the balances of payments resulting from their exchanges.

To be sure, an end to the Gold Exchange Standard without severe shock, the restoration of the Gold Standard, as well as the complementary and transitional measures which will be indispensable and, in particular, the negotiation of international credit on this new basis, all this must be examined among countries and, in particular, among those countries to whom their economic and financial power confers a particular responsibility. Besides, the appropriate frameworks for these studies and negotiations already exist. The International Monetary Fund which was instituted in view of insuring the solidarity of currencies would offer an appropriate terrain of encounter, inasmuch as it would no more be a case of perpetuating the Gold Exchange Standard but indeed of replacing it. The Committee of the Ten which, as you know, is composed independently of the United States, Britain, France, Germany, Italy, of Belgium and the Netherlands, and besides of Japan, Sweden, and Canada—the Committee of the Ten could prepare the necessary proposals; and, finally, it would be up to the six countries who appear in the process of effecting an economic community of Western Europe— it would be up to them to elaborate among themselves and promote outside a solid system which would be akin to common sense and which would correspond to the renascent economic and financial power of our ancient continent. France as far as she is concerned is ready to actively contribute to this grand reform which imposes itself (as necessary) in the interest of the entire world.

# EXCERPTS FROM DE GAULLE'S PRESS CONFERENCE OF 27 NOVEMBER 1967

## De Gaulle on France's Economic and Social Policy

In industry, where the goal is competitiveness without any reservation inside the Common Market and broad competitiveness on the world scale: to promote the investments that modernize its equipment; to encourage and help it to concentrate and improve its management methods, thus giving dimension and strength to its firms; to foster the exports and investments abroad that extend its field of action. The fact is that, over the past eight years, French industrial production has grown by an average of 5½% per annum and that industrial exports have just about trebled.

In agriculture, which must become one of the modern foundations of our economy: to induce the farms to live and work, no longer for the mere subsistence of the families that cultivate them, as in the past, but indeed for the supply, sale and purchase of the products that can make them profitable; to encourage groupings whose goal is to organize production, selection and markets to that end; to improve structures by acting to enlarge holdings that are too small, to facilitate retirement, conversions, redeployment, mergers and re-parceling. The fact is that, over the last eight years, budgetary aid to agriculture has multiplied by ten. It is likely that, at our present rate of progress, there will be one million five hundred

128

thousand farms left in France in ten years' time and that the great majority of these will be at least economic, employing 10% of our working population instead of 55% at the end of the last century and still producing altogether three times more than at that period.

In the advanced activities, which bring on and speed up production and productivity—namely research, the atom, electronics, aviation, space, television, etc.—it is a fact that, over the last eight years, the State has been making a massive contribution, which this year is eight times larger than in 1958 and which it firmly intends to increase in the future as a priority.

Naturally, there is no invention, no computer, no machine that can do away with human effort as the basis of human achievement. Men are needed for men to progress. There must be many of them, for, as regards France, all the possibilities of her territory have not yet been, and must still be, developed. This is why the growth of our population must be our prime investment, and why we are constantly led to take new measures to give more and better help for the flowering of our young French families. Also, our working population must, as far as possible, be distributed rationally between the tasks according to the needs of the national activity, and all must be suited to their employment. This means that vocational training must be extended and improved for both young people and adults, including cadres and managements; it is known that the public policies pursued to this end are using ten times more resources than they did eight years ago. It also means that student guidance must be decisively organized within national education, and this will soon be done. Furthermore, in the very considerable and inevitable major evolution of all our activities, labor and workers must enjoy security, despite necessary changes in jobs and places of work, and public aid is now being used for this purpose in all sorts of forms, whether on the national or the regional scale.

Lastly, inside firms, the direct participation of employees in the results, capital and responsibilities must become one of the French economy's basic features. A very vast social transformation in which profit-sharing, now prescribed by law, represents an important stage.

Progress, like happiness, exists only by comparison. In our industrial era, our country made a very late start compared with some others, as regards development. For a hundred years, it underwent the most terrible national ordeals and, in addition, it is relatively rather poorly endowed in natural resources—energy and raw materials. Yet the fact is that in the free world—Europe, America, Asia, Africa—we are in third place as concerns the value of our gross national product. The United States and Germany are ahead of us in this respect. Among the great industrial countries, we come second, after the United States but before Germany, Great Britain, Italy, Japan, etc., in terms of the value of our national product per capita; this is also a gauge of our standard of living, which has risen by an average of 50% over the last eight years. The fact is that the yearly growth rate of our productivity is 4½% on average, which is less than in Japan and Italy and as much as in Germany, but more than in the United States and Great Britain.

The fact is that, apart from America (whose population is four times larger than ours) and a single other Western European country, we have more research workers—40,000—than any other State and our achievements in our advanced activi-

APPENDIX 131

ties—the atom, the most sophisticated reactors (rapid-neutron reactors, for instance), the Caravelle, tomorrow the Concorde, the Diamant rocket, color television, etc.—are known the world over; this is why we contemplate without alarm the disappearance of all customs duties within the Common Market. True, we are faced with an American take-over of some of our enterprises, but we know that this is largely due, not so much to the United States' organic superiority as to the dollar inflation which they are exporting to other countries under cover of the "gold-exchange standard." It is rather remarkable that the total of the annual American balance of payments deficits over the last eight years is precisely the total of American investments in the Western European countries. There is obviously here an artificial and unilateral external factor which weighs down upon our national heritage, and France is known to wish that this abuse be brought to an end in the interest of the whole world, even in that of the United States, for whom payments deficits and inflation are deplorable, as they are for everybody.

Possibly, the storms that are now breaking forth without France being in any way to blame for them, and which have swept away the exchange rate of the Pound and are threatening that of the dollar, may finally lead to the restoration of the international monetary system based on the immutability, impartiality and universality which are the privileges of gold.

These, taken as a whole, are our goals and results as far as our economic policy and social advancement are concerned. People will say that this is self-satisfaction. No, we are not completely satisfied, and this for a very good reason: because it is in the very nature of our time that, whatever one does, one can always do more and do better. But, considering what we are achieving amongst the nations, we believe that the levers we are using are those best suited to us, and these levers are: free enterprise, which must not be a bulwark for immobility but must, on the contrary, be a foundation for impetus, for risk and for development; international competition which demands constant improvement of us; leadership, not to say "dirigisme," which selects the goals and the means, marshals resources and harmonizes efforts. This is why the Plan, in which the conditions for our progress are regularly set and coordinated, has become a vital institution in our country.

## De Gaulle on the Developments in the Middle East

The establishment between the two world wars—for it is necessary to go back that far—of a Zionist home in Palestine and then, after the second world war, of a State of Israel, aroused a number of apprehensions at the time. One could indeed wonder, and even many Jews wondered, whether the implantation of this community on lands acquired under more or less justifiable conditions and in the midst of Arab peoples who were thoroughly hostile to it was not going to lead to constant and interminable frictions and conflicts. Some even feared that the Jews—hitherto scattered but who had remained what they had been throughout the ages, namely an elite people, self-assured and dominating—might, once they were gathered on the site of their former greatness, come to change into a fervent and conquering ambition the very moving hopes they had entertained for nineteen centuries.

Yet, despite the variously rising and receding tide of ill-will which they provoked, which more exactly they aroused, in certain countries and at certain times, a considerable capital of interest and even of sympathy had accumulated in their favor, especially, one cannot but say so, in Christendom;

a capital that sprang from the vast memory of the Testament, was nourished by all the sources of a magnificent liturgy, was maintained by the commiseration inspired by their ancient misfortune which found its poetic expression in our country in the legend of the Wandering Jew, was increased by the abominable persecutions they suffered during the Second World War and, since they had recovered a homeland, was enhanced by their constructive work and the courage of their soldiers.

This is why, independently from the vast contributions in money, influence and propaganda received by the Israelis from Jewish circles in America and Europe, many countries, including France, viewed with satisfaction the establishment of their State on the territory recognized them by the Powers, whilst hoping that it would succeed, by using a little modesty, in finding a peaceful modus vivendi with its neighbors.

One must say that these psychological factors have changed somewhat since 1956. Indeed, following the Franco-British Suez expedition, a warlike State of Israel, determined to enlarge itself, was seen to emerge. Then, its policy of doubling its population through the immigration of new elements suggested that the territory it had acquired would not be sufficient for long and that, to increase it, Israel would be led to use any occasion that would arise. This in fact was why the Fifth Republic freed itself vis-à-vis Israel from the very special and very close ties forged with that State by the previous régime and applied itself, on the contrary, to fostering détente in the Middle East.

Of course, we kept up cordial relations with the Israeli Government and even supplied the arms it asked to buy for its potential defense, but, at the same time, we repeatedly urged moderation on it, in particular over the disputes involving the Jordan waters or the skirmishes that periodically opposed the two sides' forces. Finally, we refused to give our official endorsement to its establishment in a sector of Jerusalem which it had seized, and we kept our Embassy in Tel Aviv.

On the other hand, once the Algerian affair was concluded, we resumed with the Arab peoples of the Middle East the same policy of friendship and cooperation that had been France's for centuries in that part of the world, and which reason and feeling dictate that it must today be one of the fundamental bases of our foreign action.

Naturally, we did not hide from the Arabs that, to us, the State of Israel was a fait accompli and that we would not allow it to be destroyed. One could thus imagine that the day would come when our country could be of direct assistance in the conclusion and securing of a real peace in the Middle East, provided that no new drama came to tear it apart.

Unfortunately, the drama did come. It had been prepared by a very great and constant tension resulting from the scandalous lot of the refugees in Jordan and also from threats of destruction repeatedly hurled at Israel. On 22nd May the Aqaba affair, regrettably created by Egypt, offered a pretext to those who dreamed of coming to blows. To avoid hostilities, France proposed to the three other Great Powers, as early as 24th May, to forbid, jointly with them, either party from resorting to armed action.

On 2nd June the French Government officially declared that, in the event, it would lay the blame on whoever would be the first to resort to armed action, and this was what I repeated very clearly to all the States involved; it was what I had personally said on 24th May to Mr. Eban, Israeli Minister of Foreign Affairs, whom I saw in Paris.

"If Israel is attacked," I told him then in substance, "we shall not allow it to be destroyed, but if you attack we shall condemn your initiative. Admittedly, despite the numerical inferiority of your population, considering that you are much better organized, much more concentrated and much better armed than the Arabs, I have no doubt that, if this happened, you would win military successes, but later you would find yourselves involved in growing difficulties locally and from the international point of view, all the more so since war in the Middle East cannot fail to increase a deplorable tension in the world and to have very unfortunate consequences for many countries, so that it is on you, having become conquerors, that the disadvantages would gradually come to be blamed."

We know that France's voice was not heard. After attacking, in six days of fighting, Israel captured the objectives it wanted to reach. Now, it is organizing in the territories it has taken the occupation that cannot occur without oppression, repression, expulsions, and a resistance is forming against it which, in its turn, it is describing as terrorism. True, for the time being, the two belligerents are observing more or less precariously and irregularly the cease-fire prescribed by the United Nations, but it is perfectly obvious that the conflict is only suspended and that it cannot be solved, except through international channels. But such a settlement, unless the United Nations themselves tear up their own Charter, must be based on the evacuation of the territories taken by force, the end of all belligerency and the mutual recognition of each State involved by all the others. After which, through decisions of the United Nations, in the presence and under the guarantee of their forces, it would probably be possible to settle the exact outline of the frontiers, the conditions of life and security of both sides, the lot of the refugees and minorities and the terms of free navigation for all, in particular in the Gulf of Aqaba and the Suez Canal.

In France's view, if this were to happen, Jerusalem should receive international status.

For a settlement to be implemented, there would have to be the agreement of the Great Powers, which would ipso facto entail that of the United Nations; and if such an agreement were to see the light of day, France is prepared in advance to render political, economic and military assistance on the spot in order that the agreement might be effectively applied. But one cannot see how any agreement could emerge—not fictitiously on the basis of some hollow formula, but effectively for common action—so long as one of the greatest of the Four will not have disengaged itself from the odious war it is conducting elsewhere. For everything is related in today's world. Without the Vietnam drama, the conflict between Israel and the Arabs would not have become what it is, and if tomorrow South-East Asia were to see the return of peace, the Middle East would soon recover it, as a result of the general détente that would follow such an event.

# De Gaulle on the Major Objectives of Franco-Quebec Cooperation

It was the French who discovered, peopled and administered Canada for two-and-a-half centuries until 1763. When, 204 years ago, the royal Government, which had suffered serious set-backs on the continent and could therefore not pursue the war against England in America, decided to leave, 60,000 French had settled in the St. Lawrence Basin. Subsequently, their community received only minimal new elements from our country, and this at a time when millions and millions of British immigrants, recently relayed by new Slav, Mediterranean, Scandinavian, Jewish, Asian arrivals whom the Ottawa Canadian Government led to become anglicized, were settling down throughout the territory. Furthermore, the British, who since that time had controlled the power, administration, army, money, industry, trade, higher education in Canada, had naturally for long exerted great efforts to compel or seduce the French Canadians to renounce being themselves. In addition to this, there began the enormous expansion of the United States which threatened to engulf the country's economy, characteristics and language in the American mold. Lastly, France, absorbed as she was by numerous continental wars and political crises, took no interest in her forsaken children and only kept up insignificant relations with them. Everything thus seemed to be combining to submerge them in the end.

Well, by what can only be called a miracle of vitality, energy and loyalty, the fact is that a French nation—a piece of our people—is manifesting itself today in Canada and claiming the right to be recognized and treated as such. The 60,000 French left over there long ago have become more than 6 million and are still more French than ever. In Quebec itself, they are four and a half million, that is to say the overwhelming majority in that vast province. For generations, these people of peasant stock, humble farming folk, multiplied magnificently to withstand the rising tide of the invaders. At the cost of unparalleled efforts, around their poor priests, with "Je me souviens" for their motto, they struggled on and succeeded in keeping their French language, traditions, religion and solidarity. But now, they are no longer content with this passive defensive and they mean to become masters of their own destiny, like any other people; all the more eagerly since they now feel subordinate to the others, no longer just politically, but also economically.

Indeed, in view of the rural, isolated, inferior position to which the French community was relegated, industrialization occurred, as it were, over their heads—and industrialization, there as everywhere, governs modern life. Therefore, even in Quebec, the Anglo-Saxons were seen to be providing the capital, the employers, the managers, the qualified engineers, training much of the working population to their ways and to serve their enterprises, in short, disposing of the country's resources. This preponderance, combined with the Ottawa Canadian Government's policy, which was called "federal" but was inevitably partial, placed the French in an increasingly inferior position and exposed their language, their substance and their nature to growing dangers. They were far from resigned to this, all the less so since belatedly but vigorously, they were putting themselves in a position to shoulder their own development. For instance, the young people now coming out of their modern universities and new technical colleges feel perfectly capable of developing their country's great resources, and even, without ceasing to be French, of taking part in the discovery and development of all the things to be found in the rest of Canada.

All this means that the movement of emancipation that has seized the French people across the Atlantic is entirely understandable, and also that nothing is more natural than the impetus which is making them turn at the same time towards France. In the last few years, a powerful political current has formed in Quebec, which is admittedly expressed in various ways, but is unanimous as to the determination of the French to take their affairs in hand. The fact is there and, of course, they regard the mother country no longer simply as a very dear memory, but as the nation whose blood, heart and spirit are the same as theirs and whose new power is particularly suited to help their progress, while, conversely, their success would bring considerable support to France in her progress, cultural expansion and influence. Thus, in particular, the fact that the French language will win or lose the battle in Canada will weigh heavily in the struggle that is being waged for it from end to end of the world.

It was therefore with great joy and great interest that the Government of the Republic received the Quebec Government in Paris, as represented by its successive leaders, M. Lesage and M. Daniel Johnson, and concluded with them initial agreements for joint action. But this rediscovery of one another by France and French Canada obviously had to be solemnly recorded and celebrated on the spot. This was why M. Daniel Johnson asked me to pay a visit to Quebec and why I went there last July.

Nothing can give any idea of the immense wave of French faith and hope that swept through the whole people on the passage of the President of the Republic. From Quebec to Montreal, all along the 250 km road bordering the St. Lawrence and which the French Canadians call "Chemin du Roy" because, long ago, their forefathers had hoped for generations that a French Head of State would one day drive along it, millions of men, women and children had gathered to shout fervently "long live France." And these millions were waving hundreds and hundreds of thousands of Tricolor and Quebec flags, to the almost total exclusion of any other emblems.

Wherever I stopped, with the Quebec Prime Minister and one or other of his colleagues beside me, and was welcomed by elected local representatives, the crowd greeted my words with unanimous enthusiasm when I expressed three patent facts: firstly, "you are French," secondly "as such, you need to be your own masters," lastly "you want Quebec's modern expansion to be yours." After which, everyone would sing the Marseillaise with indescribable feeling. In Montreal, the second French city in the world and the last stop on my journey, the onrush of liberating passion was such that France had the sacred duty to respond to it through me, solemnly and unequivocally. I did so, stating to the multitude gathered round the City Hall that the mother country is not forgetting her Canadian children, that she loves them, that she intends to support them in their efforts for emancipation and progress and that, in return, she expects them to help her in the world of today and tomorrow. Then I summed up by crying "long live free Quebec," thus raising the fervor of resolve to its highest point.

Indeed, what is at stake is that Quebec should be free. At the point where things stand in the irreversible situation demonstrated and accelerated by public feeling at the time of my visit, it is obvious that the national movement of the Canadian French, together with the balance and peace of Canada as a whole, the future of our country's relations with the other Communities of that vast territory and even the world's now enlightened conscience—all this requires that the question be solved.

This involves two conditions. The first entails a complete change of the present Canadian structure resulting from the Act granted by the Queen of England a hundred years ago, which created the "Federation." In my view, this will inevitably lead to Quebec's accession to the rank of a sovereign State in control of its national existence, as are so many other peoples and States throughout the world, even though they are not so valid or even so populated as this one would be. Naturally, this State of Quebec would have to settle with the rest of Canada, freely and on an equal footing, the terms of their cooperation in order to master and develop a very difficult natural environment over immense expanses and to withstand penetration by the United States. But one cannot see how things could work out otherwise and, furthermore, if they work out in this way, it goes without saying also that France is entirely willing to have the best possible relationship with a Canadian entity that would assume this new character. The second condition on which the solution to this great problem depends is that the French community's solidarity on both sides of the Atlantic be organized. In this respect, things are going well. The next meeting in Paris, we hope, between the Quebec Government and the Government of the Republic should give even stronger impetus to this great French task, essential in our century. In addition, all the French of Canada who do not live in Quebec, and of whom there are one and a half million, will have to take part in this task under conditions still to be settled. I am thinking in particular of those 250,000 Acadians established in New Brunswick and who have also maintained a most moving loyalty to France, her language and her soul.

In effect, all of us French, whether from Canada or from France, can say, as Paul Valéry wrote a few days before his death: "What has been done during so many centuries of searching, misfortune and greatness and which is running such great risks, at a time when the law of the greatest number rules, must not perish. The fact that a French Canada exists is a comfort to us, an element of inestimable hope. . . . This French Canada asserts our presence on the American continent. It shows what can be our vitality, our endurance, the value of our toil. To it we must pass on what is most precious to us, our spiritual wealth. Unfortunately, too many Frenchmen have but a very vague and scant idea of Canada." And Paul Valéry concluded: "In this it is only too easy to find cause for criticizing our educational system." What would he have said of our press had he lived long enough to read all the things so many of our newspapers have published— haven't they?—on the occasion of the visit paid by General de Gaulle to the French people of Canada?

Come now! For them also, for them especially, France must be France.

## De Gaulle on Bringing Great Britain into the Common Market

Ever since there have been men and States, every great international project has been surrounded with attractive myths. This is perfectly natural, for at the root of action there always lies inspiration. And this applies to European unity. How fine and good it would be if Europe could become a fraternal and organized entity, where all the peoples would find their prosperity and security. It is true of the world also. How wonderful it would be if all differences of race, language, ideology, wealth, all rivalries and all the frontiers that have always divided the world disappeared.

But yet, however sweet the dreams, the realities remain, and, depending on whether one reckons with them or not, politics can be quite a fruitful art or a vain utopia.

Thus, the idea of joining up the British Isles with the Economic Community formed by the six continental States arouses wishes everywhere, which are ideally quite justified, but the question is whether this could be done today without tearing apart, without breaking up what exists. Well, it so happens that Great Britain, with really extraordinary insistence and haste, on some of the reasons for which the recent monetary events may perhaps throw a little light, proposed that negotiations be opened without delay between herself and the Six with a view to her entry into the Common Market. At the same time, she stated her acceptance of all the arrangements governing the Community of the Six, which seemed somewhat at variance with the request for negotiations. For why negotiate over clauses which one would have accepted entirely in advance? In fact, this was the fifth act of a play in which Great Britain's highly varying attitudes to the Common Market have followed one another without apparent resemblance.

Act one was London's refusal to take part in the elaboration of the Rome Treaty, for it was thought across the Channel that it would lead nowhere.

Act two displayed Great Britain's rooted hostility to the building of Europe as soon as it began to take shape. And I can still hear the notice served upon me in Paris as early as June 1958 by my friend Mr. Macmillan, then Prime Minister, who compared the Common Market with the Continental Blockade and threatened to declare at least a tariff war on it.

Act three consisted of a negotiation conducted in Brussels by Mr. Heath for a year and a half. A negotiation aimed at making the Community bow to Great Britain's conditions and which ended when France called her partners' attention to the fact that the goal was not this, but precisely the opposite.

Act four, at the beginning of Mr. Wilson's Government, was marked by London's lack of interest in the Common Market, the continued presence around Great Britain of the six other European States forming the Free Trade Area and a great effort to tighten the Commonwealth's internal links.

And now act five was being performed, in which Great Britain, this time, was applying for membership and, in order to be accepted, was embarking on a course of every imaginable promise and pressure.

This attitude is really quite easy to explain. The British people can doubtless see more and more clearly that, in the great movement which is carrying the world, faced with the enormous power of the United States, the growing power of the Soviet Union, the resurgent power of the continentals, the new power of China, and keeping in mind the increasingly centrifugal trends that are appearing in the Commonwealth, the structure and norms of Britain's activities and even her national personality are now at stake. And furthermore, the serious economic, financial and monetary difficulties with which she is at grips make her aware of this day by day. Hence, within herself, a tendency to seek a framework, even a European one, that would help her to save, to safeguard her own substance, that would enable her still to play a leading role and lighten part of her burden.

In this there is nothing in principle which is not salutary for her and which could not be, in a short time, satisfactory for Europe, providing that the British people, like those whom they wish to join, are willing and able to subject themselves to the fundamental changes that would be necessary for the country to settle in its own equilibrium, for what is needed is a modification, a radical transformation of Great Britain, to enable her to join the continentals. This is obvious from the political point of view. But today, to speak only of the economic field, the report communicated on 29th September by the Brussels Commission to the six Governments show absolutely clearly that the Common Market is incompatible with Great Britain's economy as it stands, in which the chronic balance of payments deficit is proof of its permanent imbalance and which, as concerns production, sources of supply, credit practices and working conditions, involves factors which that country could not alter without modifying its own nature.

The Common Market is also incompatible with the way in which the British feed themselves, as regards both the products of their agriculture, subsidized to the highest degree, and the foodstuffs purchased cheaply everywhere in the world, particularly in the Commonwealth. This rules out the possibility that London may ever really be able to accept the levies laid down by the financial regulation, and which would be a crushing burden on Great Britain.

The Common Market is further incompatible with the restrictions imposed by Great Britain on exports of capital which, on the contrary, circulates freely among the Six.

The Common Market is incompatible with the state of Sterling, as once again highlighted by the devaluation, together with the loans that have preceded and are accompanying it; also the state of Sterling which, combined with the Pound's character as an international currency and the enormous external debts weighing on it, would not allow the country to be part of the solid, interdependent and assured society in which the Franc, the Mark, the Lira, the Belgian Franc and the Florin are brought together.

Under these conditions, what would be the outcome of what is called Great Britain's entry into the Common Market? And if one wanted to impose it, in spite of everything, it would obviously mean breaking up a Community that was built and operates according to rules which do not tolerate such a monumental exception.

Nor could they tolerate the introduction as one of its leading members of a State which, owing precisely to its currency, its economy and its politics, is not at present part of the Europe we have begun to build.

To bring in Great Britain, and therefore to start negotiating now to that end, would mean for the Six—everybody knows what is involved—giving their consent in advance to all the artifices, delays and make-believe liable to conceal the destruction of a structure built up at the cost of so much toil and amidst so many hopes. True, though recognizing the impossibility of bringing the Great Britain of today into the Common Market as it stands, one might wish all the same to sacrifice the latter to an agreement with the former. Theoretically, indeed, the system now practiced by the Six is not necessarily the only practicable one for Europe. For instance, one can imagine a free trade area stretching over the whole western part of our continent; one can also imagine some kind of multilateral treaty comparable to the one that will emerge from the Kennedy Round, regulating mutual tariffs and respective quotas between ten, twelve or fifteen European States. But in either case, one would first have to abolish the Community and disperse its institutions. And I say that France is certainly not asking for this. Yet, if one or other of her partners made such a proposal, as is, after all, their right, France would examine it with the other signatories of the Rome Treaty. But what she cannot do is embark now with the British and their associates on a negotiation which would lead to destroying the European structure of which she is a part.

This would in no way be a course that could lead to the building of Europe by itself and for itself, so as not to be under the dependence of an alien economic, monetary and political system.

In order that Europe may counterbalance the immense power of the United States, it must not weaken, but, on the contrary, tighten the bonds and rules of the Community.

Certainly, those who, like myself, have proved by their deeds their exceptional esteem, attachment and respect for Great Britain, strongly wish to see her one day make her choice and accomplish the enormous effort that would transform her. Certainly to make matters easier for her, France is fully prepared to enter into some arrangement which, under the name of association or any other, would as from now promote trade between the continentals on the one hand and the British, Scandinavians and Irish on the other. Certainly, Paris is far from unaware of the psychological evolution which seems to be taking shape among our friends across the Channel, or from under-estimating the merit of certain measures they have already taken and of others they are planning, to restore their balance at home and their independence abroad. But, for the British Isles to be really able to tie up with the continent, a very vast and very deep transformation is still needed. Therefore, everything depends, not by any means on a negotiation which would set the Six on a course to surrender, thus ringing the knell of their Community, but indeed on the determination and action of the great British people, which could turn them into one of the pillars of European Europe.

## De Gaulle on Post-Gaullism

There is always an end to everything. Everyone comes to an end. For the time being, this is not the case.

In any event, "after de Gaulle" may happen this evening, or in six months, or in a year. It may happen in five years, since that is when the mandate entrusted to me under the Constitution expires.

But if I wanted to make a few people laugh, or others groan, I would say that it could equally well last another ten or fifteen years.

Frankly, I do not think so.

After the constitutional instability in which France was thrown for so long—we had 17 régimes in 177 years; after the permanent government crisis under the parliamentary régime —under the Third Republic, from 1920 to 1940, 47 Governments in 20 years, and under the Fourth, from 1946 to 1958, 24 Governments in 12 years; after the disastrous reign of the parties, displaying throughout the years, and however worthy the men may have been, its powerlessness to settle the very great and moreover very difficult problems imposed on us by our time, turning our country into what was called the "sick man of Europe," collapsing in 1940 in the tragedy of foreign war, then in 1958 on the brink of civil war and bankruptcy, it happened that the French people, acting on the proposal I put before it, endowed the Republic by a massive vote, by a tremendous majority, with solid institutions that are suited to our times.

Indeed, for nearly ten years now the French Republic, instead of offering as in former times the permanent spectacle of its Government's impotence, is on the contrary setting an example of solidarity, continuity and efficiency that is recognized everywhere and thanks to which it obtains, in the essential fields called progress, independence and peace, results which the world considers conclusive.

Apart from the partisans, nobody doubts that, if no world drama comes to call everything into question in the next few decades, the Fifth Republic will secure for France the best possible chances of prosperity, strength and influence and that, if the storm were to break out again on earth, it alone would be capable of shouldering the country's destiny.

Everyone knows that the capital feature of its institutions is that it confers on the Head of State, elected by the people, the means and responsibility for representing, asserting and if necessary imposing, over and above all particular and passing trends, the nation's higher and permanent interest. And everyone knows that, in order for policy to be consistent with what is essential, it falls to him to choose the Government, determine its composition and preside over its meetings.

Naturally, there is a wish to destroy this keystone, whether among the partisans of all kinds who, although they claim the contrary, are forever seeking to make power the stake of their ambitions and machinations, or among the conspirators of the totalitarian undertaking who aim to establish their crushing and sad dictatorship over France.

And lastly, everyone knows that if ever the President were to default in his duties, thus providing an opening for these assailants, the political and social confusion, the economic, financial and monetary deterioration and the international decline that would result would inevitably place France under the sway of one or other of the two main foreign Powers.

However, one may think that the present situation which, in specialized circles, is still arousing so much prejudice against the institutions, will not last forever. As the Fifth Republic lasts and will last, we shall probably see the vast majority of French citizens lose interest once and for all in the fruitless quarrel sought with a régime which they, in fact, have formally adopted, to which they are adjusting very well and whose dignity, solidarity and efficiency they value, whatever the passing disputes.

One may even think that, correlatively, any parliamentary combination will come to terms once and for all with the effective separation of powers which the laws and usage do not allow one to transgress.

In short, the day will no doubt come when our Constitution, with all that it entails, will have become as second nature to us. In any case, and whatever happens, it is the President of the Republic, the Head of State, who is responsible for upholding the spirit and terms of the institutions and for guiding France's policy throughout the time when he alone is the mandatory of the entire French people.

# INDEX